D0981171

THE RIGHT ROMANCE
IN MARRIAGE

THE RIGHT ROMANCE IN MARRIAGE

by
Cathy Rice

With Introduction by Dr. Bill Rice

Sword of the Lord Publishers

Murfreesboro, Tennessee

Copyright, 1966
The Right Way in Marriage for Women

ISBN 0-87398-711-X

Revised Edition April 1968

Printed and bound in the U. S. A.

During a Colorado campaign, my husband threatened to throw me away. But since I "practice what I preach" about marriage—he didn't!

Table of Contents

List of Illustrations   Page

BOOKS AVAILABLE FROM
THE BILL RICE RANCH
Murfreesboro, TN 37130

BY DR. BILL RICE

Maid of Bethany
Don't Be a Baby
Noel, the Lovin' Lion
Cowboy Boots in Darkest Africa
Brother Super
The Wonderful Word of God
Land of Beginning Again
Love 'em, Lick 'em and Learn 'em
Marriage—Husbands and Wives
Those Orangey-Red Britches

BY DR. CATHY RICE
From My Heart

BY OTHER AUTHORS

The Story of the Bill Rice Ranch—by Pete Rice
Dr. Bill Rice—"I Like You!"—by Bill Rice III
Things a Millionaire Can't Afford—by Dr. Russell Anderson
    (Hardback or Paperback)
Darkness Is Light—by Dr. Billy Renstrom
Singing in Signs. . .(Song book for the deaf)
Signing for Jesus. . .(A Workbook)

I CALL HER THE PRINCESS

INTRODUCING THE AUTHOR
By Her Admiring Husband,
Evangelist Bill Rice

I believe this book will do great good. For the past several years the Princess has taught these lessons to women who have attended some of this country's largest Bible conferences that are conducted here on the Bill Rice Ranch each summer. And we have received more letters of appreciation, from both men and women, concerning these lessons than from any other one feature of the conferences. She has also taught these lessons in many cities where she has accompanied me for revival campaigns, in Bible institutes and Christian colleges.

I'll tell you one thing—the gal who wrote this book has certainly made a rip-roarin' success of her own marriage! We have been married for twenty-nine wonderful, wonderful years. And at the risk of sounding like a love-sick school-boy—I love her more than I love everything and everyone in this whole world put together!

TWO AS ONE

You will notice, in this book, that Cathy is great on stressing the fact that husbands and wives should become "one flesh." And I suppose the two of us really have become "one" more nearly than any two people I have ever known. This may be a little surprising since the environment of our "up-bringing" was so different.

She was brought up in a happy Christian home in a big

city. This home was considerably above average in refinement, culture, income and Christian standards. My parents, too, were stalwart Christians and I enjoyed a fine, happy home until orphaned in my teens. But I was brought up in small towns and ranches in cattle country. By the time I was twenty-one years of age I had probably taken about as many baths in a washtub as a bathtub, my idea of classical music was hound dogs singing on a rabbit trail, and I thought napkins were something used only on Sundays by women and preachers! I was twenty-one when I met Cathy. She was one of the "Widner twins" and I went to hear them sing on the radio. I walked up the stairs in Dallas' Blackstone Hotel because I thought you had to pay to ride the elevator!

And yet, how wonderfully our lives have been blended together to become "one."

COMPANION FOR FUN

As for a "for fun" companion, I would rather have her with me than anyone in the world. Because I love hunting and camping and ranch life and animals, she does, too. On her golden horse, Tinklepaw, she sometimes joins me on rides around the ranch. The animals, whether tame ones like horses and dogs, or wild ones like coons and deer, seem to instinctively trust and love her.

I once bought her a small pistol but she never has become a very good shot with it. I will say this, though—she shoots differently from most women. As a rule, a woman will aim a gun and then close her eyes and pull the trigger. The Princess, however, closes her eyes *first*—and then aims and pulls the trigger!

A "HELPMEET" FROM HEAVEN

She is not only a wonderful companion but a tremendous helper in the work God has called us to do. She faces most things with enthusiasm; all things with courage and resolution!

We have known abject poverty. In fact, I honestly do not know any preacher who has been as poor as Cathy and I. When we were first married I made about six dollars a week as pastor of a small Baptist church! The Negro maid in her father and mother's home had a larger salary than I. And the allowance she had received from her parents for just spending money was more than this. Yet she made the transition smoothly and without complaint. Hard times hit that first winter and we lived mainly (I am serious about this) on turnips! We ate those things boiled, fried, stewed, baked and raw! We ate 'em whole, halved, diced and mashed! And the love and cheerfulness of the Princess was just as great then as it was eighteen months later when the little church had grown to seven hundred members and our salary had been multiplied by twelve!

This matter of taking things as they come has been one of her finest characteristics. She has learned, like Paul, *"In whatsoever state I am, therewith to be content."*

She has lived sacrificially without feeling like a martyr. When we attended Moody Bible Institute in Chicago we lived in dark, damp basement rooms where we had to contend with everything from cockroaches to drunks. She made our little room bright with the radiance of her cheerfulness and love. And through the years, as our growing ministry has taken us to many places in far-off lands, she has been equally at home in humble hovels and palaces.

She has always had a wonderful knack of budgeting her time. When we were graduated from Moody we had two little girls. Within the next couple of years we had two little boys also. And since I was gone from home so much of the time in revivals, it was up to Cathy to run the household largely by herself. Soon I needed a part-time secretary but we could not afford one. So she bought a ninety-eight-cent book on how to type and spent a few dollars on books that taught Speedwriting. (Shorthand.) Within six weeks she was taking dictation and typing efficiently.

A bit later I needed, but again could not afford, a good pianist for special revivals. She had taken piano lessons as a girl and now she bought a couple of books on evangelistic piano playing and was soon an above-average revival pianist!

Still later it was decided that she and the four children should travel with me all the time in revival campaigns. She bought school textbooks from the famous Calvert courses, set up classrooms in every revival and spent the mornings teaching the children. It was not until they were ready for high school that they were enrolled in the public schools. (Betty, being deaf, was an exception. She traveled with us only during the summer months.)

SHE BELIEVES GOD

Her simple faith has been a real inspiration to me again and again. When we were graduated from Moody I felt definitely that God wanted me to be an evangelist. My famous big brother, Dr. John R. Rice, put an announcement in *The Sword of the Lord* that I was out of school and available.

I expected a flood of invitations for revivals. No flood came! In fact, it didn't even rain. To be more truthful—it didn't even sprinkle! Finally, I received one invitation and I didn't know what to do. I had been working at the Railway Express and wondered if I should give up a good job in order to accept just one revival invitation. But the Princess settled that quickly.

"Does God want you to be an evangelist or an express-man?" she asked. When I answered that God wanted me to be an evangelist, she put her arms around my neck and smiled, "Then what's the problem?"

Put that way—there wasn't any! I resigned my job and, a few days later, hightailed it for Indiana and that first revival campaign!

Then there was the time, fifteen years ago, that I felt someone should start a nation-wide missionary work to the deaf. I contacted the leading preachers in a number of denominations but could not sell any of them on sending out workers to the deaf. One day the Princess and I were driving home from a revival in Florida and I was complaining that I couldn't get anyone interested in the fifteen million deaf in this country although this was one of the largest mission fields in the entire world, with a wide-open door.

Finally, as we drove along, the Princess put her arm around me and said, "Don't you know who the Lord is going to use to start a missionary work among the deaf?"

"No, I don't," I replied.

"Well," she said, "I know who is going to do it."

"If you do know," I said, "I sure wish you would let me in on the secret."

"You are going to do it," was her surprising reply, "and I am going to help you."

"Great guns, Princess," I complained, "how in the world can I do it? I am not anybody, I don't have any money, I don't have any prestige—I don't even belong to any convention of any kind. How in the world do you think we could begin a mission work to the deaf?"

To this she had a simple and unanswerable reply. "I have heard you preach many times," she said, "that if God lays a burden on *your* heart, then He expects *you* to do something about it. And a person *can* do anything God *wants* him to do."

Now, just about the worst thing that can happen to any man is to have his own wife preach his own sermons back to him! But a few months later we made a down payment on an old, worn-out ranch in Middle Tennessee, put up a couple of small open-air cabins and invited twelve deaf boys and girls to spend a week with us.

That was fifteen years ago. The work has grown until it is now, by far, the largest missionary work to the deaf in the entire world! We not only have hundreds of teen-agers visit the ranch each summer but the Princess teaches courses in Sign Language each year to both home and foreign missionaries. There are probably more Protestants working among the deaf in the United States today who were taught Sign Language by her than by those who were taught by everyone else combined!

SWEETHEART

However, when all is said and done, it is as a sweetheart that I treasure my wife the most. After all, a preacher can hire a secretary, an evangelist can hire a pianist, a father can even hire someone to take care of his children. But if there is to be romance and intimate love in a man's life—that must come from his wife! And a wonderful, warm, tender, loving sweetheart she has been to me. Physically, she is just as attractive today as she was the day we were married. As a matter of fact, she is even the same shape and weight she was then! She keeps herself neat and clean and fresh and dainty.

Yesterday I returned home after a week of meetings in Denver. As the big jet came in for a landing in Nashville, I could hardly wait for the wheels to hit the runway. I look forward to being with the Princess again with as much eagerness and excitement as I had experienced on our wedding day!

I agree with Solomon that *"A virtuous woman is a crown to her husband."*

And surely the Lord had one like Cathy in mind when he had Lemuel to write:

"Who can find a virtuous woman? for her price is far above rubies. The heart of her husband doth safely trust in her, so that he shall have no need of spoil. She will do him good and not evil all the days of her life....Her children arise up, and call her blessed; her husband also, and he praiseth her."

*To my lovely mother
Lelah B. Widner*

*There is no doubt in my mind
but that my mother's marriage has
been wonderful because she has
followed the principles outlined
in this book. She not only taught
me well, but was and is a living example to me in "The Right
Romance in Marriage."*

Chapter 1

The Right One in Marriage

"Whoso findeth a wife findeth a good thing, and obtaineth favour of the Lord."—Prov. 18:22.
"Who can find a virtuous woman? for her price is far above rubies."—Prov. 31:10.

MARRIAGE

Marriage is the oldest institution in the world and God intended it to be a happy one.

At this point a couple is at the door of Heaven or the gates of Hell. The new life they are entering can be a life of sublime happiness but it may be a life of sheer boredom or even misery.

I remember my mother saying before Bill and I were married, "Be sure you love him. It is hard enough to live with a man you love. Living with one you did not love would be hell on earth."

Next to our conversion, marriage is probably the most important step we will ever take. But, to look around and see the misery and unhappiness in so many homes makes us realize how frivolous so many girls are when it comes to marriage. Many fail to consider the seriousness of it and plunge into it carelessly and heedlessly.

I realize that many a girl, fearing she might be an old maid, marries the first fellow who comes along to save herself from this predicament, only to live in regret the rest of her life. Others, living in an unhappy home caused by fussing or perhaps poverty, feel they can marry and get away from this. But they find instead of stepping into a life of sublime happiness they have only jumped from the frying pan into the fire.

Marriage in itself does not make happiness.

Just because you are a good Christian does not necessarily mean you will have a happy marriage—not even if the man you marry is a good Christian. And just because your parents are happily married does not guarantee your marriage will be happy.

Happiness in marriage is something that must be worked for in order to be achieved. It is something that must be earned.

How much better it would be, then, to wait for God's leading and to marry *"in the Lord."* Marriage is so important, it should never be misused or abused. Yet of all institutions, it seems to be the most misunderstood.

THE RIGHT ONE FOR ADAM

God created Adam and placed him in the beautiful Garden of Eden. Adam had all the animals in the world to love, to pet and to keep him company. Yet God could see that Adam was lonesome.

In Genesis 2:18 we read, *"And the Lord God said, It is not good that the man should be alone; I will make him an help meet for him."*

God saw that it was not good for man to be alone, and He knows the same about us. God knew that Adam had the beasts of the fields, the fowls of the air and the fish in the sea at his beck and call. But God also knew these could not fulfill the heart or physical needs of Adam. None of these were *"meet"* for him.

God had created a man who needed a wife!

God said it was not good that man should live alone, even

With my husband in Nazareth, Palestine. Because Bill is an evangelist, he must do a great deal of traveling. Since I am part of him, I do a a great deal of traveling, too.

though in a garden of beauty—animals, birds, fish and every living creature—so God made a *"help meet"* for Adam.

God knows the same about us. He knows that loved ones are dear to us and that friends mean a great deal to us. But He also knows that each of us has a need for a special someone to fulfill a natural longing that has been in the heart of every person since the creation of Adam.

Brothers, sisters, mother and father and friends are important to us, but no bond on earth should be as strong as that of a man and woman in holy matrimony.

In Genesis 2:21-25 we have the beautiful story of how God caused a deep sleep to fall upon Adam and, as he slept, the Lord took his rib and made a woman.

(Adam actually paid for his wife by the blood of his own

side. Here we have the first picture of Christ whose side was pierced for His bride—those of us who are saved.)

Eve became a new creation. God then brought this lovely, beautiful creature, made especially for Adam, and gave her to him.

Adam and his rib were brought together again and he was so happy and pleased that he said, *"This is now bone of my bones, and flesh of my flesh."*

Here God performed the first marriage ceremony. Right here God made the pattern, the perfect example for us all. He said, *"Therefore shall a man leave his father and his mother, and shall cleave unto his wife: and they shall be one flesh"* (Gen. 2:24).

FINDING THE RIGHT ONE FOR YOU

Since marriage is a divinely ordained institution of God, surely God would make some rules or plans for us to follow in this all-important matter.

He does—and those who heed what God has to say are sure to find the *right one* for themselves.

There are four things any woman should consider in finding the right husband.

1. Pray for the Clear Leading of the Lord.

No Christian should ever enter into marriage without the clear leading of the Holy Spirit. I doubt if one person out of a thousand, or even ten thousand, prays, "Lord, show me the *right one* to marry."

You should certainly pray for wisdom to recognize and know when the right one does come along. James 1:5 reminds us, *"If any of you lack wisdom, let him ask of God, that giveth to all men liberally, and upbraideth not; and it shall be given him."*

The Lord will help you in this. I know, for I have seen it work dozens of times. Remember that God is interested in the right one for you and the right one for your children. Marriage should not be entered into without the clear leading of the Lord. Speaking of widows, I Corinthians says she may marry again, *"only in the Lord."* So this should be for all Christians who marry *"only in the Lord."*

The time to pray is *now,* before you have fallen in love with the wrong person.

(Right here let me say a word to parents: the time for parents to pray is when the children are small—not after they are grown and engaged to be married.

A mother in Augusta, Georgia, asked me to pray for her lovely, talented daughter, explaining that the girl was soon to be married. The mother felt, though the young man was saved, her talented daughter who was a good musician should be marrying a preacher or someone in gospel work.

I asked her if she was praying about this and she assured me that she certainly was. She prayed day and night that the girl would wake up and not be so foolish as to marry this young fellow.

I then asked her how long she had been praying and she answered, "Oh, ever since she became engaged—several weeks now."

I told her I would pray for the daughter but I doubted if it would do much good. After your children have fallen in love and become engaged is too late to begin to pray. They should have been praying through the years as the child was growing up.)

And pray for patience to wait for that right one. I'm afraid too many are so anxious to be married and are afraid they will be passed by that they marry the wrong one. But I have seen those who patiently waited for God's choice and time—and how glad they are!

Our own deaf daughter, Betty, is a wonderful example of this. She is a lovely, beautiful girl and several fine young men proposed to her. Yet she waited until she was past twenty-five before she married.

There was one young deaf man whom my husband and I felt sure Betty would fall in love with and marry. He seemed to be everything that a girl could want in a husband. An outstanding scholar and athlete, he had graduated with highest honors from his school. While still in his early twenties, he had secured a fine job that paid him almost three times an ordinary salary. He dressed well, drove a large new automobile, had flawless manners and was, according to Betty, a perfect gentleman.

When he began courting Betty, he drove several hundred miles every weekend to Murfreesboro. Here he rented a hotel room and visited with Betty Saturday afternoons and evenings and went to church with her Sunday mornings.

One night, however, Betty came in and announced that the young man would not be back again. With surprise and astonishment we asked why. She replied, "He says he loves me and wants to get married. But I could never love him. I feel God wants me to marry someone in full-time gospel work. He's a Christian and a fine man but I told him tonight not to come back. He is looking for a wife and I told him I would never marry him. I thought he ought to know that he is making the long trip and spending all of this money for nothing!"

When Betty had her twenty-fifth birthday she cried and cried. She said, "Mother, you and Dad taught me that if I would pray and have patience God would send the right one along. Why doesn't He?"

I felt heartsick, for I knew her distress. I could only answer that although I could not understand why the right man had not come along, I still knew God does not lie. And if God did not have someone for Betty to marry, He had something better for her.

Six weeks later Betty went to Tennessee Temple College in Chattanooga and one of the first persons she met was Don, a handsome young ministerial student who felt called of God to work with the deaf! They fell in love and were married and Betty says now, "I'm so glad I waited."

2. You Are to Be One Flesh.

Genesis 2:24 says, *"Therefore shall a man leave his father and his mother, and shall cleave unto his wife: and they shall be one flesh."*

God made the man and the woman for each other and they became as *"one flesh."* It is important to remember that you and the one you marry are to be as one. Do you fit perfectly in every way with the one you are planning to marry? If not, then he is NOT the *right one* for you. You should be as much a part of your husband as your hand is a part of your body. If you know there are things that will keep you from becoming one flesh, then now, before it is too late, you had better pray for God to give you strength and courage to give up your sweetheart. Pray for strength to wait for the *right one.*

No verse in all the Bible says that three or four shall be one flesh. God gave Eve to Adam and then said, *"They shall be one flesh."*

Jesus endorsed this Genesis account of the creation of man and woman for each other as one flesh when He said:

"Have ye not read, that he which made them at the beginning made them male and female, And said, For this cause shall a man leave father and mother, and shall cleave to his wife: and they twain shall be one flesh? Wherefore they are no more twain, but one flesh. What therefore God hath joined together, let not man put asunder."—Matt. 19:4-6.

God made one woman for Adam. The Bible never condones more than one wife for one man. Wicked men living in a wicked civilization have sometimes changed this. But even godly men of old did wrong by having more than one wife. These men sinfully fitted into the pattern of their times.

Moreover, divorce is wrong although it has become a way of life in modern America. Today, even many Christians are divorced. But this is wrong. They have sinned in fitting into the pattern of our times.

In I Timothy 3 there is a discussion of the qualifications of a pastor and deacon that should properly fit all Christian men. In verse 2 and again in verse 12 it is mentioned he should be *"the husband of one wife."*

3. For Life.

Marriage is to be for life. Think seriously about your sweetheart. Is he one you will enjoy living with 365 days a

Riding a camel, the ship of the desert, in Cairo, Egypt

year? year in and year out! The Bible plainly teaches that marriage should never be broken except by death. The only legitimate reason for divorce recognized by the Bible is continued adultery, or fornication.

First Corinthians 7:39 says, *"The wife is bound by the law as long as her husband liveth; but if her husband be dead, she is at liberty to be married to whom she will; only in the Lord."*

Matthew 19:6 says, *"What therefore God hath joined together, let not man put asunder."*

Marriage is a lifetime relationship. It is contrary to God's plan for marriage to end in divorce.

Marriage is the most beautiful picture God Himself knew to illustrate Christ and the church. We see this in Ephesians 5:23,31 and 32:

"For the husband is the head of the wife, even as Christ is the head of the church: and he is the saviour of the body. . . . For this cause shall a man leave his father and mother, and shall be joined unto his wife, and they two shall be one flesh. This is a great mystery: but I speak concerning Christ and the church."

God hates divorce and all Christians should have a desire to please their Heavenly Father and to want to walk in paths that would please Him.

The marriage vows should be all-important. When you marry, the words spoken should not be taken lightly. When you say, "for better, for worse, for richer, for poorer, in sickness and in health," and to "honor and obey," you should mean this with all your heart. This is a covenant you make with your life partner and this means that no matter what the circumstances, no matter how hard or how easy it may be, you are vowing to stick to the end.

To break this vow makes you a liar. The time to find out if the man you are marrying is mean, will beat you, will not respect or love you, will never attend church, etc., is before marriage.

And, incidentally, young woman, you should not try to hide anything from the man you plan to marry. If you are lazy, a poor housekeeper, have a sharp tongue and do not plan to be his sweetheart forever, you will regret it if you keep these things hidden from him until after you are married!

Remember, then, marriage is for life. The time to consider whether or not you intend to live up to your marriage vows is before—not after—you take them!

Sometime ago *The Sword of the Lord* published a thought-provoking story that I believe is worth reprinting here.

LET'S REWRITE THE MARRIAGE VOWS
By Dr. Don W. Hillis

There I was, walking slowly down the aisle to the lovely strains of Lohengrin's wedding march. I was wearing the most beautiful bridal dress and veil any doting parents could give their only daughter. The church was artistically decorated and I held in my arms an exquisite bouquet of roses. Tim stood at the altar, tall, handsome and happy. Warm bursts of excitement and love flooded my whole being as he took my arm at the front of the church.

Then in quiet, sober tones the pastor commenced to speak. After a brief message on the importance of love in the husband-wife relationship, he began to pronounce the wedding vows. That was when it happened. All at once I realized what I was doing—the commitments I was making. The unreasonableness of it shook me. The horror of it gripped my heart and filled me with fear.

The pastor was saying, "Beth, will you take Tim to be your wedded husband, to live together according to the ordinances of the church in the holy estate of matrimony? Will you obey him and serve him, love him, honor him, and keep him in sickness and health, in poverty and wealth, and forsaking all others keep yourself only for him as long as you both shall live?"

All at once I knew I shouldn't say, "I will." All at once a thousand reasons why I should say, "No," flooded through my mind. Anyone of a dozen things could happen to Tim in the first twenty-four hours of our married life which would make the next forty years a living nightmare. Why hadn't I thought of this before—why was I making such irrational promises to any man? But there I was and what should I do but say, "I will"?

The pastor then asked me to repeat the following words after him, "I, Beth, take you, Tim, to be my wedded husband, to have and to hold from this day onward, for better, for worse, for richer, for poorer, in sickness and health, to love, cherish and obey till death...."

I blacked out at that point. Several of the women uttered muffled screams as I sank to the floor. It was all a fake on my part, but it looked real. I had to have time to either change or rethink the wedding vows. As Tim tenderly lifted me in his arms and carried me out of the church, I heard the pastor say, "Friends, I'm sorry about this, but I'm sure Beth will be all right in a few hours. She has been working hard and is, no doubt, overly tired. We will complete the wedding in the home of her parents when she is feeling better. Perhaps it will be just as well for it to be a private ceremony."

As Father, Mother and I sat around the breakfast table the next morning, I started the conversation. "I'm terribly sorry about yesterday," I said. "I know you were disappointed and even mortified, but I had to do something about those wedding vows. They have to be changed. It's not right to ask any girl to make such promises to any man. I'm supposed to love Tim as long as I live more than I love you or anyone else on earth, regardless of what happens to him or of what he turns out to be."

My father couldn't hold in check his horrified reaction. "Beth, if you marry Tim or any other man whom you do not love enough to make such promises gladly—you are not my daughter."

Mother's reaction was more restrained. She said, "I see your point, Beth. There are many things which could happen to either you or Tim which would produce some real hardships and problems in your married life. Perhaps it would be well if we rewrote the marriage vows."

With pencil in hand, Mother began to write: "I, Beth, take you, Tim, to be my wedded husband, to have and to hold as long as you are well and strong, to forsake when sickness comes along, to love and cherish when I feel like it, to obey when it is to my advantage, to serve as long as you maintain a living standard commensurate with my desires, and, forsaking all others, I will keep myself for thee only, until a better man comes along."

"Stop it!" I snapped.

"Yes, dear," Mother replied, then added, "there is one thing more unreasonable than getting married within the unqualified bonds of sacred matrimony—that is, to get married apart from a love which wholeheartedly accepts those bonds."

"I guess you're right," I stammered. "It would be foolish to get married if your wedding vows were filled with 'ifs' and 'buts.' I wouldn't want Tim's promises to me filled with conditions."

"Daddy and I have enjoyed twenty-four wonderful years together," interrupted Mother. "It was our unqualified love for and unconditional commitment to one another which have made our married life delightful."

All at once I wanted to enter into that same supremely happy entanglement my parents had been enjoying for so many years. A telephone call to Tim—repentance, tears, forgiveness, and a mutual, unqualified confession of love for one another—brought it about. And how lovely it is to be Tim's wife—how exciting to love him, honor him, and keep myself only for him!

4. Agreement.

Amos 3:3 says, *"Can two walk together, except they be agreed?"*

You cannot find two men working together in harmony if they are not in agreement. Countries go to war because of lack of agreement. And marriages break up for the same reason.

Two cannot walk together as one if they do not have mutual interests, the same outlook on life, the same spiritual views, the same desires, etc. How important it is that a man and woman who plan to marry agree.

Christians should marry only Christians. Second Corinthians 6:14-16 says:

"Be ye not unequally yoked together with unbelievers: for what fellowship hath righteousness with unrighteousness? and what communion hath light with darkness? And what concord hath Christ with Belial? or what part hath he that believeth with an infidel? And what agreement hath the temple of God with idols? for ye are the temple of the living God; as God hath said, I will dwell in them, and walk in them; and I will be their God, and they shall be my people."

How can two people live together in harmony day and night when one is saved and the other unsaved? Their thoughts and ideals are as far apart as the east is from the west, as far as day is from night. Usually when a believer marries an unbeliever, the believer's heart is turned away from the Lord. King Solomon was the wisest man that ever lived, yet his heart was turned away from God by his pagan wives.

"And he had seven hundred wives, princesses, and three hundred concubines: and his wives turned away his heart. For it came to pass, when Solomon was old, that his wives

turned away his heart after other gods: and his heart was not perfect with the Lord his God, as was the heart of David his father."—I Kings 11:3,4.

Being married to an unsaved one is bound to lead to sin, heartache and much unhappiness. It is bound to bring the judgment of God. The flood came because the "sons of God married the daughters of men." The yoke of marriage is the closest and longest-lasting agreement you will ever make. I have read in several books, "If a child of God marries a child of the Devil, he is certain to have trouble with his father-in-law." The unhappiness brought on by the unequal yoke not only brings unhappiness to the man and woman, but to the children born to this union.

Christians who marry the unsaved usually find their joy gone, testimony gone and usefulness to Christ gone.

Many a Christian girl marries an unsaved man feeling because he is so wonderful and their love so strong that she can reform him after the marriage ceremony. Such a marriage rarely turns out well. Any reforming that is to be done should be done before marriage.

Real problems come in a marriage when one is Protestant and the other is Roman Catholic. To marry a Catholic you must have two licenses—one from the state and one from the Catholic Church. The latter will not be given until the non-Catholic has signed away her right to bring up the children in her church. The child must be brought up as a Catholic. A child belongs to both parents but the Roman Catholics say that the child belongs to the church. This can only bring heartache and sorrow.

I would even go so far as to say that a girl should marry a man of the same religious denomination. A Baptist should marry a Baptist, a Methodist a Methodist, a Presbyterian a Presbyterian. Even the mode of baptism, which can be fun to discuss before marriage, can become a sore spot after marriage.

I probably thought more seriously about marriage than most girls. My father and mother were and still are happily married but so many of my girlfriends' parents were not. Why? I often wondered about this.

As I sat pondering the question one day, the thought came to me that a girl certainly needed to pray about her marriage, and then have enough patience to wait until the right man came along. But how would I know the right man?

That day I wrote down what I would expect to find in my ideal man. I have kept that list to this day and I share it with you now.

MY IDEAL MAN

In searching for my lover and mate I look for, in him, the following characteristics:

1. He MUST be a Christian.

2. He MUST be truthful.

3. He must be stable, standing on his own feet with plenty of hard, solid backbone and a mind of his own.

4. He must be brave. Never a coward, cheat, sneak or one to mind the other fellow's business. Never to be a bully to run over the weak and small but always ready to help those less fortunate than he.

5. He must be a good sport.

6. He must not be idle, spending his time loafing about poolrooms, drugstores, etc., but be a man who finds useful ways of spending all his time.

7. He must be a leader among men. By this I mean one who can make his influence felt; not one that always follows.

8. He must have high regard for women—above all, his sweetheart and wife.

9. He must have ambition.

10. He must have an appreciation for good music, art and literature.

11. He must not be a fanatic on any one subject.

12. He must not use profane language or have a temper he is unable to control.

13. He must not drink or smoke.

14. He must be a man, not a sissy.

15. He must be nice looking, neat and tidy in dress, clean inside as well as out.

16. He must be able to understand me in all my ways.

17. He must be dependable; one that I can put all my faith, trust and confidence in; one I will be happy to confide in.

18. He must have faith, trust and confidence in me and be willing and glad to confide in me, who will let me share all his trials and troubles.

19. A man that will let me be his dearest friend, chum and pal on earth; who will let me walk hand in hand with him to his goal.

20. He must love me with all heart and soul and receive the same love from me in return.

(Signed) Mary Catherine Widner
1933

As I read this now I realize I had my sights high. But when I met Bill and we had been friends for a while, one day I read the above and said to myself, "You know what? I believe he fits everything on that list."

And today, after thirty wonderful years together, he fits it even more. How good it is to be in love with my ideal man.

Chapter 2

The Right Plan in Marriage

"Therefore shall a man leave his father and his mother, and shall cleave unto his wife: and they shall be one flesh."
—Gen. 2:24.

"Wives, submit yourselves unto your own husbands, as unto the Lord. For the husband is the head of the wife, even as Christ is the head of the church: and he is the saviour of the body....Husbands, love your wives, even as Christ also loved the church, and gave himself for it."—Eph. 5:22,23,25.

REAL RESPONSIBILITIES

Being sure you marry the right one is so important. But that would be to no avail if you did not have the right plan after you were married. Many young couples seem so fitted for one another—their love is so radiant and romantic—but it is short-lived. Let a few months pass and they are bickering and fussing like "old married folks."

What causes this change? Why has bitterness and bickering taken over in place of love and admiration? What makes a marriage turn sour?

Walking down the church aisle amid orange blossoms and greenery to be joined in holy matrimony to the one you love with all your heart is sheer ecstasy. You feel in your heart that here is perfect love, the perfect marriage. But there is more to it than "they lived happily ever after." Good marriages don't "just happen," but a happy, successful marriage is an achievement.

Before our daughter Kaye's first baby was born, she had to have a cyst removed. I went to Memphis to be with her. Since Kaye was five months pregnant, they had her in the maternity ward.

Charles, Kaye's husband, is a Marine, so Kaye was in a Naval hospital. The ward was full of young brides of sailors, most of them with their first babies.

I sat there in the evening and watched the proud young sailors as they came in to see their brides and new babies. I watched these young couples as they walked, with love in their eyes, arm-in-arm down the hall to the nursery. But I could not help but think that in a few years the happy marriage would be over for some of these couples.

The romance of a beautiful wedding with a tenor singing "I Love You Truly," or even the thrill of a new baby, is not enough to guarantee the success of a marriage.

A successful marriage is something that must be earned day by day.

NOURISHED AND TENDED

A woman can plant a rose garden but it does not just grow by itself. God sends the sunshine and the rain but unless it is tended and cared for, it will not flourish. Weeds will come up and soon take over. Bugs will come and destroy the tender young plants. If the woman is to have a garden that is to mature and become a thing of beauty, she must work at it continually.

And so it is with marriage. Even if it is a marriage *"in the Lord"* with His "showers of blessings and smile of sunshine," it will not stand if those to whom it has been entrusted do not tenderly and lovingly care for it.

Marriage is a real responsibility and young folks who are not ready to take on the heavy responsibilities are not ready for marriage. Make sure you are ready for these responsibilities before taking them on.

After you marry, you have someone other than yourself to think about. When Bill and I married, my father reminded us that I was Bill's to clothe, feed and care for. And I

My husband and I at the tomb of Christ in Jerusalem

realized that I must face certain responsibilities, too, in order to be the kind of wife that would make and keep my husband happy. Then soon "little responsibilities" are added!

Just as you can find God's plan for the *right one* in marriage, so you can have the *right plan* for a happy marriage as found in God's Word.

I understand that it takes both husband and wife to make

this plan work right. But you should do your part whether your husband does or not.

A woman once said to me, "I try to do right but my husband won't, so what's the use?" But two wrongs do not make a right. You do right and good will follow. Don't wait for your husband.

We are free to violate God's laws but we are not free from the effects of our transgressions!

THE RIGHT PLAN

1. One Flesh.

Remember from the last chapter we learned that you are to be as one person with the one to whom you are wed. You should be so much a part of one another that, like Adam, you can say *"bone of my bones, and flesh of my flesh."*

I'm sure you have noticed how a couple, who are deeply in love and have been married a long time, even seem to look alike!

God's ways are perfect and it seems we would want to follow His leading but the Devil puts it into the hearts of all of us to be rebellious. How foolish we are! God instituted marriage and He has a plan for marriage that is *just right*. Look how beautiful it is.

God's loveliest creation is woman. God made her from an actual part of Adam. God knew that it was not good that man should live alone and that he needed a "help meet." That means someone that was suitable for him. God did not make Eve from a rock or a tree or an animal, but from part of Adam's body.

What part of Adam? Not his head, for she was not to rule over her husband. Not from his feet, to be a slave or to be trampled upon. But God made her from a rib taken from Adam's side near his heart. So a wife is to be ever near her husband's heart, part of him, a help meet to be loved and cherished and closer to his heart than any other person.

A dear lady said to me at the funeral of her husband, "My husband was a good friend to me." But a wife and husband should be far more than "good friends." She should be as close to him as if she were actually part of his body.

No one ever hurts his own flesh deliberately. Notice Ephesians 5:28 and 29, *"So ought men to love their wives as their own bodies. He that loveth his wife loveth himself. For no man ever yet hated his own flesh; but nourisheth and cherisheth it, even as the Lord the church."*

No person ever sets out to deliberately injure his body. What kind of person would bite or kick or scratch himself! We would think such a person crazy.

In Mark 5 is the story of the maniac of Gadara who was always crying and cutting himself and no man could tame him. Not until the unclean spirit was removed by Jesus did the man care for himself.

It is natural to protect our own bodies. So should we be careful of our lovers. It is surprising to me, however, how often husbands and wives seem to delight in hurting one another. But God said you are to be *"one flesh."*

2. Live Together.

In Genesis 2:24 God said, *"Therefore shall a man leave his father and his mother, and shall cleave unto his wife: and they shall be one flesh."* And in Matthew 19:5 Jesus said also that a man was to leave his father and mother and cleave to his wife.

So a young couple marrying should *leave* parents and *cleave* to one another.

A girl gives up her own name and gets a new name that she should wear with pride. Any woman who wants to hang onto her maiden name is not doing right. She ought not want to keep her old name but should proudly take the name of

her husband. Look at the Hollywood glamour girls. They
want to marry but stay as they were, without taking on a
new way of life.

A girl leaves her home with mother and father, to begin a
new home with her husband. Rebekah was willing to leave
all—home, friends, loved ones—and live in a far country
with her husband. Girls should be willing to leave all and
follow their husbands. They should say, *"Whither thou
goest, I will go; and where thou lodgest, I will lodge: thy
people shall be my people, and thy God my God,"* as Ruth
said to Naomi, her mother-in-law. (Ruth 1:16).

You are to start a new life—his home, your home; his
people, your people.

If his people are not the kind you want to be your people,
then you had better not marry him. If his home is not the
kind of home you want, then you had better not marry him.
You are to leave the old and cleave to your husband.

But you will notice—it is to the man that God gives the in-
junction to cleave to his wife. The Bible does not say that
a man is to live with mother and father—but that he is to
leave his mother and father and *cleave* to his wife!

A boy keeps his name, has the same job and goes about
more or less the same as before, but with a wife added. But
a man needs to realize, "Now I am married and my wife
must be first in my life from now on. She comes before my
father or mother, brothers or sisters, friends or loved
ones."

I have often heard my husband say when preaching on the
"Home" in revivals that it is the boy's mother who seems to
cause the most trouble for the newly married, feeling the
girl just does not know how to properly care for her "baby
boy"! She often feels that the girl cannot cook good enough,
does not know how to sew, or keep the house, or even to
properly iron her boy's shirts.

But, according to the Bible, the husband is to see to it that his parents do not make life miserable for his bride. He is to leave mother and father and take his lovely young wife as she is.

There may be many things a young bride will need to learn how to do in order to please her husband. But he must have patience with her and, above all, must not throw his own mother up to her continually.

When a couple start their married life, it is better that they begin it by themselves. The old saying that no house is big enough for two families is right. Couples should start alone even if in a little crackerbox room. I know that sometimes circumstances make it so that the young marrieds must live with some of their folks, but this is not best and should never be any longer than necessary.

This does not mean that the new couple should ignore their parents. They should seek wise counsel from them and have a warm family relationship on both sides. But always remember, they are starting a home of their own. The in-law problem has disrupted many a marriage. In fact, in-laws are a major cause of more than 65% of all divorces. And the "in-law" that figures in more than 55% is —you guessed it—the husband's mother!

A girl should never consider running back to mother, and a boy should be free of his mother's apron strings.

3. Man to Be the Head.

"In the day that God created man, in the likeness of God made he him."—Gen. 5:1.

A man is like God in a sense that woman is not like God. God is masculine. God is always called "He" in the Bible. He is called Father, the Son, the Bridegroom, the King, etc. Christ's body was a man's body on earth. So man, made in the likeness of God, is fitted for things that a woman is not fitted for.

Notice that the Bible plainly says the husband is to be the head of the home!

"For the husband is the head of the wife, even as Christ is the head of the church: and he is the saviour of the body."—Eph. 5:23.

"Unto the woman he said, I will greatly multiply thy sorrow and thy conception; in sorrow thou shalt bring forth children; and thy desire shall be to thy husband, and he shall rule over thee."—Gen. 3:16.

Men are to be the head of the home and lead in love. *"... as Christ also loved the church, and gave himself for it;... so ought men to love their wives."* In this picture the wife is not a slave or hired servant but the man is to love her as Christ loved the church. He is to woo her and captivate her by his love. And he, as the head, is to protect, guide and lead his wife and family in the paths of righteousness.

The husband will want to fashion his love for his wife after the love of Christ for the church. Christ's love was a sacrificial love—*He "gave himself for it."*

So a husband's love should be so deep and strong and sacrificial that he would be willing, if need be, to lay down his life for his wife's sake. He must make her first in his thoughts and in his heart.

Christ's love also provides for the needs of His own. So the husband should sincerely desire to take care of his wife and to fulfill even her slightest need. And he must want to do more than supply the need for clothing, food and a house to live in. He should also want to fulfill her emotional, mental and spiritual needs.

As Christ's love never wavers for us, so a husband's love should never waver for his wife.

A strange thing happened once when my husband was conducting a revival campaign in Canada. One night a man came to me and said he would like to ask me a question which his wife had been wanting to ask but was afraid to. He said, "Do you really do everything your husband asks you to do? Do you really obey him in everything?" (My husband had just preached a sermon on "The Home.")

I looked at him, grinned and said, "Well, yes I do. But it is not as bad as you make it sound. My husband loves me and is always more than kind and good and considerate of me. I cannot imagine him wanting me to do anything that would not be good and right and the best for both of us."

Later, in our motel, I was telling Bill about it. He sat thinking for a few minutes, then said, "You know what? If that man had asked me if I did everything you wanted me to do, I'd have answered 'Yes!'"

And that is right; he would. We love one another, and each of us want to do our best to make the other happy.

I do not mean that Bill is not the head of our home, for he certainly is. I just mean that he leads our home with love, and I would not have it any other way.

4. Man to Lead His Home.

As head of his home, a man should realize his great responsibility and lead his wife and family in the right way. Joshua said, *"As for me and my house, we will serve the Lord."* This is what every Christian husband and father should say.

Many people feel that men must "sow their wild oats" — that they are more wicked than women and therefore it is up to the wife to lead in church matters. Some people have the idea that it is not as bad for a man to enter into sin as it is for a woman. But this is a lie from the Devil. Eve was the first one to take of the forbidden fruit but Adam was the one God called and questioned!

God intends that the husband should set the spiritual pattern for the family.

The world has a way of setting one list of standards for women and girls and another for men and boys. But man as the head and leader should not expect those who follow him to go one way while he goes another.

Lot made that foolish mistake. The Bible says that he was a *"just man."* But he did not live like one and he did not lead his family in the right way. Instead, Lot *"pitched his tent toward Sodom"* and as a result, lost his wife, two married daughters and ruined his two single daughters.

God holds a man responsible for leading his family in paths of righteousness. He should take the lead in church attendance, Bible reading, daily family prayer and in winning the children to Christ.

5. Wife to Be in Subjection.

"Likewise, ye wives, be in subjection to your own husbands; that, if any obey not the word, they also may without the word be won by the conversation of the wives."—I Pet. 3:1.

"Wives, submit yourselves unto your own husbands, as unto the Lord."—Eph. 5:22.

Subjection means to yield to the authority of your husband.

Ephesians 5:33 says, *"And the wife see that she reverence her husband."* A wife is to reverence her husband, that is, to love and respect him.

God made woman to be a *"help meet."* A help meet stands with her husband in victory, in defeat, in sorrow or in joy. She is part of him and ever at his side. It is said that behind every great man there is a woman to help and sustain him. Sometimes this is his mother but more often his wife. A woman who takes her place in sweet subjection of love can become a great blessing in the life of her husband.

First Timothy 3:11 gives the qualifications for a pastor's

wife but these should be for all Christian wives. *"Even so must their wives be grave, not slanderers, sober, faithful in all things."*

God made Eve for Adam to be his assistant. God made Adam first and then a helper for him. Not a partner, not a "boss," but one to be part of him. As a hand is part of the body to serve and help the body, so a wife should be to her husband.

A Christian wife is even to be in subjection to her unsaved husband. As stated in I Peter 3:1-7, you will notice that wives are to be in subjection to their own husbands even when they *"obey not the word"*—and that they by their *"conversation"* (way of life) may win their husbands. Read these verses and notice that God's value of a Christian wife is *"of great price."*

6. Prayer and Bible Reading.

In Joshua 24:15 Joshua said, *"As for me and my house, i will serve the Lord."*

When a man and woman are united in marriage, Christ should be in the center of their lives. This makes matrimony holy.

When a man and woman pledge their lives to one another they need to build these lives on a solid spiritual foundation. Marriage really needs to be made in Heaven as well as on earth!

As soon as a young man and a young lady are married, a new family has begun and a new circle of prayer and Bible reading should be established. And as the children are born into the family, Bible reading and prayer should be part of the family and become part of their lives. The whole family should worship together. Prayer at mealtimes is a *must*. And prayer with the children at bedtime is blessed and wonderful. But the entire family needs to gather daily for a time of Bible reading and prayer.

A young couple should attend church regularly and take an active part. As the children come into the home they, too, should be enrolled in Sunday school and should attend church from earliest infancy.

This is God's plan for a happy marriage and it will work. If you expect your marriage to be happy, do it God's way.

On an ocean liner in the Caribbean. My husband is answering Ranch and Sword correspondence. He says he will probably die with a dictating machine in his hand! If he does, I will probably have just handed him that last letter to answer!

Chapter 3

The Right Way in Marriage

"Husbands, love your wives, even as Christ also loved the church, and gave himself for it."—Eph. 5:25.

"So ought men to love their wives as their own bodies. He that loveth his wife loveth himself. For no man ever yet hated his own flesh; but nourisheth and cherisheth it, even as the Lord the church."—Eph. 5:28,29.

"Nevertheless let every one of you in particular so love his wife even as himself; and the wife see that she reverence her husband."—Eph. 5:33.

THE WAY

Once you are married to the right one and both have determined in heart to have God's plan for marriage in the home, you are on the way. But marriage is something more than a machine to start or stop by the punching of buttons.

Even in a Christian marriage where the couple wants a good marriage, with the husband as the head and the wife in her rightful place, often something seems to go wrong. Instead of being *"one flesh"* they seem to grow farther and farther apart and their love grows cold. Instead, they should be growing more and more alike and becoming more as *"one flesh."*

And the tragic thing is that so often we see even a preacher's home wrecked and ruined by an unhappy marriage.

Once a preacher we knew came where we were and stayed long. His wife had left him and he seemed to be heartbroken. With tears he begged us to pray for his broken home.

Again and again he told us he simply could not understand

why his wife had left him. "It just happened overnight," he repeated over and over.

But I happen to know that this had not "just happened overnight." Years before this preacher's lovely little wife had talked to me about some of their problems. It seemed his life was so wrapped up in himself that he had no time for his wife nor his children. As he talked to us with tears in his eyes about his broken heart I could not help but remember the tears of his wife years before as she told me her troubles and wondered how long she could keep the family together.

My husband often receives letters that reveal to us that so many marriages are full of trouble. One man wrote, "We have been married only a short time but my wife has fallen far short of what I expected in marriage."

Although I was raised in the city, my husband was practically born in the saddle. Now that has become my way of life, too. Tinklepaw, my golden horse, and I spend many hours together.

A woman wrote, "If my husband loves me, I don't know it —he never tells me."

Another wrote that it did her good to see my husband show in public that he loved his wife and children. She said her husband acted as if she and their children were strangers to him. We hear complaints like these often—good Christian folks married and living in the same house but strangers to one another. This is tragic and heartbreaking. What goes wrong?

LOVE IS BASIC INGREDIENT

Men are admonished three times in Ephesians 5 to *"love their wives."* First, as Christ loved the church and gave Himself for it. Second, as their own bodies. Third, as themselves.

First Peter 4:8 and 9 says, *"And above all things have fervent charity [love] among yourselves: for charity [love] shall cover the multitude of sins. Use hospitality one to another without grudging."*

People often say, "Love is blind." We see a man love a woman and we sometimes wonder how in the world he could love such a person. But all agree that "love is blind." Love really does *"cover the multitude of sins."* All of us have shortcomings and are certainly not perfect, but love will cover this if we will only keep it alive.

A woman needs to keep herself lovable so that her husband will stay in love with her. Read First Peter, the third chapter, carefully and notice what it has to say about women. Magazine articles and modern psychologists would have us believe that the way we dress and keep ourselves is the most important way to keep a husband. But God's way is how we are in our hearts—not mean and corruptible, but with a meek and quiet spirit.

I know it is often hard to stay sweet and lovable when your

husband tracks in mud, throws his clothes all over the floor, makes all kinds of extra work for you and often is not very sweet himself.

But it can be done! It will be hard work, but a woman must learn to discipline herself to this. Remember, you took him for better or for worse!

So, when things go wrong, don't nag. Proverbs 27:15 says, *"A continual dropping in a very rainy day and a contentious woman are alike."*

Proverbs 21:19 and 25:24 tell us it is better to dwell in the corner of a housetop or in the wilderness than with a brawling and contentious woman in a wide house. It seems that after marriage some women change. They become naggers and are fussy and bitter and mean.

But for a man to love his wife, she must *be lovable* and *stay lovable.*

WAYS TO BE MORE LOVABLE

As the years roll by in marriage, how can we keep our love fresh and sweet?

Ephesians 5:33b reminds the wife *"that she reverence her husband."* This reverence is respect mixed with love. So, a woman with a quiet, sweet spirit and with reverence toward her husband would certainly do several things:

1. Notice Him.

Many women, after they "get the man," forget him. Their lives get wrapped up in the children, the cooking, washing and ironing and a million other things that demand the time and attention of us females. So the lover gets pushed further and further into the background.

When my children were small a woman came to me and said she felt led of the Lord to talk to me. Then she proceeded to tell me she felt I was too wrapped up in my husband. She said a woman should make her children her life while the husband made his work his life. I thanked her for telling me this but told her I just could not agree. I told her I was made to be part of my husband and that he would always be my life.

I am a twin and was born being part of someone. Perhaps that is why I felt such a need to be a part of my husband.

But that is really God's way in marriage. Then I did not know how wrong that woman was but today I do.

Just a couple of years ago this same woman said to me, "I think it is just wonderful how you and Bill are so much a part of one another." Then she went on to tell how miserable she is now because all her children are married and gone from home and her husband is wrapped up in his business and she has nothing. I could not help but wonder if the woman could remember her talk with me many years ago.

Every wife needs to remember this: You start with just you and your husband and, the Lord permitting you both to live, you will wind up right where you started! And there is no reason why your marriage should not be just as full of love and romance at the end as in the beginning.

So stay in love with your husband and you will have each other when the children leave to start their new homes.

2. Have Consideration for Him.

Cook the foods he likes, wear the clothes he likes for you to wear, keep yourself attractive for him. As you grow older this will take more time and effort but it will be time well spent.

Pet and spoil him some! Most men like this. When Bill comes home from meetings, I often serve him his breakfast in bed. When your husband comes home in the evening tired and worn from the day's work, carry him a cool glass of lemonade, or a cup of coffee and make him feel comfortable while you prepare supper. Many of us make our husbands so sour they never want to do anything for us.

One Christmas we went to Nashville to do some shopping and while we were in a store there I noticed a man and a woman. The man was buying his wife a dress for Christmas. After trying on several she decided on one. Her husband said, "I wish you would get the blue one instead of that one. I like the blue one better." Now, remember, he was buying this as a gift for his wife. But the woman hatefully replied, "I don't care what you like. I'm the one to wear it and I'll get what I like!"

I'll bet that is the last dress he ever buys her. Poor fellow, he was embarrassed to death because of her mean and hateful talk in front of a large group of shoppers.

I simply cannot understand a wife who has no consideration at all for the feelings or desires of her husband. For me, no matter how horrible the blue dress, I'd have wanted it above all others if Bill liked it.

I once read the following on being considerate toward the husband and we wives can profit from it.

If he's in a talkative mood, give him your undivided attention. If he seems preoccupied or tired, let him alone.

If you have news he isn't going to like to hear, don't spring it on him the moment he walks through the door.

Bad news will usually keep at least until dinner is eaten in peace.

If he's in a bad mood, don't make it easy for him to start an argument or hurt your feelings.

If he has had a good day and is feeling on top of the world—climb up there with him!

Point out anything you want him to notice, instead of saying accusingly, "You haven't even noticed such and such."

If he wants to enjoy a radio or television program or a good book, don't keep on chattering.

Make the dinner hour as pleasant and relaxed a time as possible.

3. Honor Him.

Make him the king of your domain. Look up to him and make him proud to be "lord and master" of such a home. So many women seem to delight in making their husbands look like two cents.

Some wives want to mother their husbands. But if you want your husband to be a real man, you had better treat him like one.

First Corinthians 8:1 says, *"Knowledge puffeth up, but charity [love] edifieth."* So learn to praise him and brag on him. A man loves to be bragged on and he had rather know his wife is pleased with what he does than any other person on earth.

Do not criticize and find fault with him. If you must do it, do it in a sweet spirit and in the privacy of your own home— never in front of other people.

Recently some people who were passing through Murfreesboro stopped by the ranch to meet us. They were in our home just a short time, but the wife still had time to criticize her husband. She told us what a horrible driver he was, how he sang too loud in the church service where they had stopped to visit on their way south, and that she was embarrassed that he continually looked at his watch all during the services.

I felt it made the man feel badly although he may have grown so accustomed to her sharp tongue that he paid no attention to it. But a wife should learn to be loyal and to point out her husband's good points, not his bad ones. She should build him up—he will get enough pulling down from the world without his wife helping to do it.

Moreover, a wife will certainly get more enjoyment out of her marriage if she is sweet and lovable to her husband than if she is mean and critical.

4. Learn to Be Courteous and Polite to Him.

Saying "please" and "thank you" does not hurt any of us but it sure helps the feelings of others. Remember, the Bible says, *"A word fitly spoken is like apples of gold in pictures of silver"* (Prov. 25:11).

It might be well to take to heart the little poem we often teach our children,

> *Hearts, like doors, ope' with ease*
> *To very, very little keys.*
> *And don't forget that two of these,*
> *Are "Thank you, sir," and "If you please."*

Before marriage you enjoyed the many little courtesies shown you by your lover: he would open the door for you, help you into the car, seat you at the table, help you on with your coat and was always thoughtful and courteous.

(After thirty wonderful years of marriage, my husband still does these things for me.)

If your husband has changed toward you in this respect, perhaps it is your fault. Doubtless you were more polite and courteous to him before marriage than you are now. Remember, courtesy, kindness and thoughtfulness are two-way streets.

5. Eliminate Needless Irritants and Antagonisms.

All of us have some things that bother the other fellow. We need to find those things which bother our husbands and get rid of them. Do not nourish feelings of resentment. Learn to talk things out and get them settled. Ephesians 4:26,27 says, *"Be ye angry, and sin not: let not the sun go down upon your wrath: Neither give place to the devil."*

Never sit around wishing you had married the other fellow. Don't get angry at the same time your husband does but control your temper at all costs.

Both man and wife need to have a good sense of humor. Colossians 3:19 says, *"Husbands, love your wives, and be not bitter against them."* Love and bitterness cannot live in the same house. Bitterness in one's heart spreads like an evil disease.

Don't be babyish and pettish about things, crying and sulking to get your own way. Put yourself in your husband's place and try to understand his attitudes, desires and feelings.

6. Make the Best of Life Together.

Maybe things will not turn out as well and as prosperous as you anticipated. But remember, you married "for better or for worse."

It has been said that one's eyes should be wide open before marriage and half-shut afterward.

The fact is, as long as the husband and wife love one another, misfortune and poverty do not seem too important, anyway.

I remember how happy Bill and I were when we were working our way through school in Chicago. We lived in a small, dark, damp, smelly basement apartment. We fought rats and mice and cockroaches and even bedbugs!

It was in the depression and jobs were hard to find but Bill sometimes worked shoveling snow—without overcoat or gloves. I found odd jobs babysitting and then working as a waitress in a restaurant.

Our clothes were shabby and patched.

And yet we were deliriously happy! We had each other and we were in the will of the Lord. Nothing else seemed to matter very much.

7. Cultivate Common Interests.

Learn to be interested in the things your husband is interested in and to like the things he likes.

If your husband likes dogs and horses, as mine does, learn to like them, too.

If you had told me before my marriage that I, Catherine Widner, would ever enjoy ranch life, I'd have said you were crazy. I was raised in a nice, citified home in Dallas and a horse was as much of a rarity to me as it is to most of you.

But today I hardly recognize myself as the same girl that grew up in that large city. Here I am a ranch gal, liking horses, loving dogs and am a regular ole ranch hand.

Bill, you see, was raised in the ranchlands of West Texas and dogs and horses and cattle were part of his life. Now they are part of my life, too—mud, dirt and all!

Bill loves horses and I, too, have found them easy to love. In fact, as I write this I am heartsick because one of the sweetest and most-loved of all our horses has just been put to sleep. She has been sick for some time now and in spite of two operations and all the vets could do, she could not recover. And it is almost as if we had lost a member of the family.

8. Cultivate a Rich, Spiritual Life Together.

As we said in the last chapter, Christ should be the center of our homes. There ought to be a time for Bible reading and prayer in the family altar.

But in addition to that, a husband and wife need to have a rich spiritual life together for themselves.

First Peter 3:7b says, *"As being heirs together of the grace of life; that your prayers be not hindered."* You do not want to be embarrassed before God when you come to pray, so you and your husband need to keep everything clean and open and on praying ground.

I love all the Ranch babies! When the men tell me of the new births I always try to visit the mother and babe at once. This golden stallion colt is precious!

9. Love Him.

Love him with all your heart and tell him so often. Love begets love and if you would let him know you love him, perhaps he would show more love toward you. Sometimes what seems to be the most beautiful and perfect marriage is in reality just a form and covers lonely and bitter hearts. But love can transform the humblest of marriages into a lovely romance "until death do us part."

Chapter 4

The Right Sex Life

"Marriage is honourable in all, and the bed undefiled: but whoremongers and adulterers God will judge."—Heb. 13:4.

"Now concerning the things whereof ye wrote unto me: It is good for a man not to touch a woman. Nevertheless, to avoid fornication, let every man have his own wife, and let every woman have her own husband. Let the husband render unto the wife due benevolence: and likewise also the wife unto the husband. The wife hath not power of her own body, but the husband: and likewise also the husband hath not power of his own body, but the wife. Defraud ye not one the other, except it be with consent for a time, that ye may give yourselves to fasting and prayer; and come together again, that Satan tempt you not for your incontinency."—I Cor. 7: 1-5.

THE BLESSING OF MARRIAGE

Marriage is the physical union of man and woman in a relationship that is only to be dissolved by death. There is more to marriage than the sex relationship but no marriage is likely to be a happy one if there is not a good and well-adjusted sex life. Marriage is a divine institution and we rightly call it "holy matrimony."

When Bill and I had been married about four years, he conducted a revival in a large Indiana city. After being there for several days the pastor's wife told me that she had done a great deal of counseling over the years with marriage problems. She said from her long and varied experiences she had learned that a man and woman who were still "in love" after several years of marriage had found the joy and sweetness of a happy sex life.

This gave me food for thought because I wanted more than anything in the world to have a happy marriage. I determined in my heart then and there that I would continue to do all I could to keep our sex relationship a good one.

GOD MADE EVE FOR ADAM

God saw that it was not good for man to be alone (Gen. 2: 18) so God made a woman for Adam. You will notice that they were male and female—

"So God created man in his own image, in the image of God created he him; male and female created he them."—Gen. 1:27.

If Adam had needed something or someone just to amuse him and keep him entertained, he had all the animals in the world. If he had simply needed someone to have fellowship with, God would have made him another man. Or, if it was just a spiritual union, Adam would have had no need for a wife or any other person because God visited with him in the garden daily.

But God knew that man needed someone for much more than entertainment or fun or even spiritual companionship. Man had a heart need and a physical need and God said it was not good for man to live without a wife.

So God made Eve for Adam because she was needed to fill the natural and God-given longing in Adam's heart and body.

GOOD AND RIGHT

Marriage was instituted in the Garden of Eden for a perfect man and a perfect woman!

"And God blessed them, and God said unto them, Be fruitful, and multiply, and replenish the earth, and subdue it: and have dominion over the fish of the sea, and over the fowl

of the air, and over every living thing that moveth upon the earth."—Gen. 1:28.

Adam had not sinned when God made Eve for him. Many people have the silly notion that it was because of sex that Adam and Eve were cast out of the garden. But this is a perverted idea. God plainly told them to *"Be fruitful, and multiply, and replenish the earth...."*

How could Adam and Eve replenish the earth if there had been no sex relationship? Not one place in the Bible are we told that it was sinful and wrong for Adam and Eve to live as man and wife. On the contrary, Hebrews 13:4 says, *"Marriage is honourable in all, and the bed undefiled."*

The mating of husband and wife is right and good. And it is pure because that is what *"undefiled"* means.

MAN AND WOMAN DIFFERENT

It seems the most misunderstood aspect of marriage is the sex relationship. Why is it that so many husbands and wives never seem to get an understanding on this point?

It is because men and women are made differently!

God made them *"male and female."* Two creatures, with bodies uniquely different, yet made to complement each other perfectly to make a well-rounded life.

Yet many a man goes through life never understanding or knowing his wife's needs or desires. Likewise, how many wives go through life never understanding their husbands.

Psalm 139:14 tells us that we are *"fearfully and wonderfully made."*

How wonderfully God made man and woman. How marvelous it is that you can grow up in the same home with a brother, eat the same foods, play the same games and you develop lovely soft skin, beautiful hips and a lovely bust while your brother develops a body that is hard, muscular and broad-shouldered.

The marvel of a man is his masculinity, and the glory of a woman is her feminity. Nothing in the world is more repulsive than an effeminate man, soft and lacking in manliness. And it is just as repulsive to see a woman with the characteristics of a man. God made us to be different and we need to take these differences into consideration.

MAN'S NEED

The Lord made man with a strong sex urge. This is a God-given hunger and is just as real as his hunger for food. This is a hunger in a man that needs to be filled. But this is normal and right and is not evil and wicked as some women seem to think.

This biological urge in a man is the cause of restlessness and wandering in teenage boys and young men until they find their mates and can settle down with them.

Bill and I on the shores of famous Galilee. A beautiful romantic place that Jesus loved.

And after marriage, if a man is not satisfied at home, he is likely to become frustrated and frantic and this often drives him to immoral and godless living.

First Corinthians 7:2 says, *"To avoid fornication, let every man have his own wife, and let every woman have her own husband."*

And in I Corinthians 7:9 we read, *"But if they cannot contain, let them marry: for it is better to marry than to burn."*

So the bodily desires of a man that press him toward marriage should result in love and gratification to keep him from temptation.

When you marry, your body is no longer your own but your husband's.

"The wife hath not power of her own body, but the husband."—I Cor. 7:4a.

When you marry, you give your body to your husband and you become *"one flesh."* You are to give yourself to him wholeheartedly that he may avoid the sin and temptation that often comes when a man is frustrated in his natural sex urge.

Remember, these are God-given desires in a man and not unclean and filthy and sinful.

A woman, telling me of her husband, said, "He is just a beast." But when I questioned her about him, I found he was a very normal man with a natural and healthy sex appetite. The woman wanted me to pray for her husband but she was the one who needed prayer and to be shown from the Bible where she was wrong.

There is nothing wrong with a man wanting his wife. But there is something wrong with a wife not gladly giving herself to her husband. Concerning this matter the Bible says, *"Defraud ye not one the other..."* (I Cor. 7:5).

"Defraud" means to deprive or cheat one of a possession, and you are your husband's possession. The sex urge in a man is normal and right and has no restriction in the Word of God. To be considerate and loving toward your husband and his need is *"your due benevolence."*

Many a woman would be spared the heartbreaking torments of seeing her husband turn to another if she could only learn to give herself completely and entirely to him. *"Defraud not"* but *"render due benevolence."*

Although a man is saved and wants to do right, he may find himself too weak to keep from entering into deep sin if his life is frustrated at home. The sex instinct is said to be stronger than any instinct except that of self-preservation. Even a good Christian man, with good intentions, strong will power and sincerely desiring to be pure in heart, may be tempted to commit adultery if he is starved sexually.

WOMAN'S NEED

A woman does not have the same strong sexual urge that a man has. But her need and her drive toward marriage is just as real and just as strong. And there is a biological urge in a woman's body, put there by God.

This urge in a woman craves the love and attention of a man. She has certain nerves and parts of her body that respond to the loving caresses of a man and in turn this creates in her a sexual desire.

The lovely, beautiful body of a woman is appealing to a man. He can look upon the body of a woman and be stirred to the depths. David sinned because he *watched* a beautiful woman bathe.

(Incidentally, this is the reason it is so important that a woman keep her body decently and properly clothed. This is also the reason mixed bathing is not good. A man is stirred with sexual desire when he looks upon the nudeness of a woman. This desire is God-given and his being a Christian does not stop this reaction. And this is exactly the reason that a man should never look upon the nakedness of any woman other than his wife.)

But a woman is different than a man. She may look upon the body of a man without lusting. While the lovely, beautiful legs of a woman can stir a man, a woman can look at the bony, hairy legs of a man and feel nothing! But when he caresses and fondles her, then desire begins to stir in her body.

Freedom of caresses and love-making and fondling are right and proper for man and wife. And all husbands need to learn and understand this need in a woman's life.

But love-making and petting is dangerous for the unmarried. As said before, the sex instinct is so strong that barriers may be broken down. When a girl allows a boy to love and fondle her body she may give way to passion and allow herself to be led into adultery when she never intended or dreamed she would do so.

Women and girls who have no respect for their bodies often lose the respect of the men with whom they pet. The principal attraction of a girl to any man is her body and men often feel that a girl who will pet will go further. Ironically, the girl who is free with her body usually thinks it will help her get a husband, when just the opposite is true. No man wants to marry the girl he feels might have committed adultery with any man she allowed to fondle her body.

GIVING YOURSELF

After marriage each partner should determine in his or her heart to learn and to understand the needs and the feelings of the other.

"Therefore all things whatsoever ye would that men should do to you, do ye even so to them...."—Matt. 7:12.

The wife should put herself in her husband's place and do for him that which will help him. The husband should, in turn, take the feelings and needs of the wife into consideration. Each rendering unto the other *"due benevolence."*

I know many women are perplexed and perhaps shocked when they are first married and feel the man they married is abnormal. But sex is of God and is meant for our happiness and our good.

A woman should enter into marriage with an open heart and she should give herself completely to her husband. The intimacies of marriage should be blessed and sweet.

And a man, to reap full benefit of his sex life, must try patiently to understand his wife. Most Christian girls are taught to have reverence for their bodies. Therefore, they enter into marriage with a modest innocence and are not fully aware of their own sex desires. They do know, however, that they want affection, loving caresses and devoted attention from the one they love. A husband should always bear this in mind. It will pay him to remember that tokens of affection such as giving flowers, perfume, dainty lingerie, with loving words and caresses, will do much to stir the romantic soul of a woman.

A woman needs time after her marriage to develop normal sex reactions and enjoyment. Oftentimes the fear of pregnancy may cause a woman to keep from giving herself completely to her husband.

(Incidentally, I never teach this subject without women asking me whether or not it is right to use some method of birth control. My husband says that God gave a general command for us to *"Be fruitful, and multiply, and replenish the earth."* If some method of birth control is used to deliberately disobey this command, then it is wrong. But if some method of birth control is used prayerfully to space the children, then there is no commandment against it.)

Then, too, a man who has such strong pressure toward intercourse, may have the mistaken idea that the girl he marries is made with the same strong biological pressures. Therefore, he may be disappointed when he marries and finds she does not. He may even feel he has married a "frigid" woman.

But he must learn to know the importance that love-making and caresses play in the sex life of a woman. Women love as fervently as men but they come to marriage with strong inhibitions and these must be removed by an understanding and patient husband.

Of course many of the wife's inhibitions will vanish when she remembers that her body now belongs to her husband. You become *"one flesh"* and should so give yourselves to each other and so mold yourselves to one another's needs and desires that you actually become one.

"The wife hath not power of her own body, but the husband: and likewise also the husband hath not power of his own body, but the wife."—I Cor. 7:4.

No intimacies should be withheld. A woman should give herself to her husband without reservation, and likewise, a man should give himself to his wife without reservation.

God made Adam and Eve. *"They were both naked, the man and his wife, and were not ashamed"* (Gen. 2:25). It is not wrong, then, that the husband and wife be naked before each other and unashamed.

SOME THINGS TO REMEMBER

1. A woman needs to remember that her body is lovely and appealing to her husband and she should keep it that way for him. As we grow older this gets harder to do. But you should do all you can to keep yourself neat and trim for your husband. Keep your body sweet smelling, your clothing

clean and nice, your hair combed and be well groomed! (Be sure your slip doesn't show!)

Keep yourself appealing to him and he is not likely to have wandering eyes for another woman.

2. Remember, a husband and wife should never let their courtship die. God made a woman very romantic by nature, so it is just as important for husband and wife to have dates after marriage as before.

It is good for a man and wife to get away from home where she will not have washing dishes, scrubbing floors and tending the babies to worry about. She needs to be a-lone with her husband where they two can enjoy one another's company without interruptions.

3. Remember, for a woman to really give herself whole-heartedly to sex, she must have her mind free of the problems of the day. She should not have to think about what she will prepare for tomorrow's meal, Junior's cut knee and the many routine things that weigh on her mind.

Then, too, a woman needs and must have privacy for complete surrender to her husband. Alone with him, they two can be lovers with no inhibitions. There should be no limit to the intimacies of married couples.

4. And the husband must always remember to show her affection and take time for caresses and kindness. A wom-an, to be a lover, must have words of love. She has a right to this as much after marriage as before. A man needs to take time to love and pet his wife if he expects her to enter freely and willingly into a happy sex relationship.

5. Remember, a man or a woman who defrauds or cheats his or her lover, will find that he or she is the loser. A woman who gives herself completely to her husband will find she gains in the long run.

By giving yourself completely to your husband, you will reap love and kindness many times over. Do not make your husband feel as if he is cheated and that something that is rightfully his is beyond his reach. Never use sex as a weapon. Never try to punish your husband by withholding yourself from him.

6. Remember, happiness in the sex relationship must be worked for to be achieved. It must be fed day by day. Keep the touch of your husband's hand as sweet and fresh to you as the years roll by as it was the first time he touched you.

Ask your husband to tell you frankly how he feels and what his needs and desires are. You, in turn, explain your desires to him. Do all you can to make him happy—give yourself completely to him and your happiness will necessarily follow.

Snapped by a sidewalk photographer at the Acropolis in Athens, Greece. My husband is always on the go and I am usually right by his side (or a half step behind!).

Chapter 5

The Right Romance in Marriage

(Get your husband to read this chapter with you.)

"Submitting yourselves one to another in the fear of God."
—*Eph. 5:21.*

"Likewise, ye husbands, dwell with them according to knowledge, giving honour unto the wife, as unto the weaker vessel, and as being heirs together of the grace of life; that your prayers be not hindered."—*I Pet. 3:7.*

It takes two to make a marriage. The husband has his part as well as the wife. It is certainly easier for a man to love and show his love for a woman when she is constantly trying to be loving and kind and thoughtful to her husband, as outlined in the preceding lessons. On the other hand, a woman's well-being, her sense of security, her happiness in life, depends on love received from "her man" more than most males ever seem to realize. Their presence can make us content, restful and give us a feeling that all's right with the world while their absence can make us cross, resentful and weary to the very marrow of our bones.

I remember years ago when our children were small and Bill was gone from home months at a time in revival meetings. As soon as he left the door the weight of the world settled down on my shoulders. As I look back now, I realize how cross and cranky I must have been with the children and others in his absence. But one day it was really brought home to me when a young woman who was living with us said, "You become a different person when your husband is gone. We can't help it because he is gone all the time and it's just not fair for you to take it out on me and your kids."

For the first time I began to realize it and I have seen it again and again, not only in myself but in other women as well.

I recently read an article about Queen Elizabeth of England in which the author said, "People of England have noticed that her charm can be more dogged than vivacious — until Philip appears."

When a woman is loved by a man, knows it and has him near, she blooms and blossoms.

MEN COMMANDED TO LOVE THEIR WIVES

The Scripture says that men ought to love their wives *"as Christ also loved the church, and gave himself for it."* That a man should love his wife as he *"loveth himself"* and as he loves *"his own flesh."*

"So ought men to love their wives as their own bodies.... For no man ever yet hated his own flesh; but nourisheth and cherisheth it, even as the Lord the church."—Eph. 5:28,29.

When my husband preaches on the home he always shows how careful a man is of a sore finger. He will be ever so careful not to hurt that finger when he gets his keys from his trousers pocket! And a man needs to be just that careful of his wife. Care for her, be mindful of her every need, protect and love her.

No man walks around jabbing himself with a needle just because he is bored or irritated or because he has nothing else to do. Why, then, should any husband—representing Christ—continually hurt his wife with sharp words or actions simply because he is out of sorts or bored?

MEN SHOULD BE CONSIDERATE OF THEIR WIVES

First Peter 3:7 says a man is to dwell with his wife according to knowledge, *"giving honour unto the wife, as unto*

the weaker vessel." In other words, the husband is to respect his wife, to be considerate of her. And Peter goes on
to say that this should be done *"that your prayers be not
hindered."* Neither God nor man has any respect for the
husband who mistreats his wife. Some men seem to feel
that they should be tyrants in the home. They mistreat and
abuse their wives and live like demons in the home instead
of being a loving, protecting provider for the sweetheart
who gave her love to him. This is so serious with the Lord
that I Peter 3:7 says such a man's prayer will be hindered.

I believe there are several things we should think about in
regard to a man's treatment of his wife.

1. It's the Little Things That Count.

Many a man seems to think he has an extremely happy
marriage when suddenly his wife announces that she is leav-
ing to make a life for herself, to return to her parents or
even to get a divorce. He just can't imagine what has happened! I even remember hearing one man say, "Why, it
just happened overnight. My wife just decided to leave
overnight."

But it didn't happen "just overnight." Things had been
piling up for years and probably most of them were "little"
things. Most males simply do not realize how important
these "little things" are to a woman.

Men seem to believe they are good husbands if they work
hard, provide a good home and plenty of food, provide the
necessary clothing, play with the children, take their wives
out occasionally and are uncomplaining.

But a woman needs so much more than these things. It
has been said that men are 75% sweetheart and 25% father,
while women are 75% mother and 25% sweetheart. Perhaps
this is true. But I am sure women would be more sweetheart if their husbands would only help them be that way.

Women are creatures of romance, and to be sweethearts they must be romanced. In other words, as long as a man lives, he needs to court, romance, dine, send gifts and make love to his wife.

When a man is courting his sweetheart, he is neat and clean in appearance, sends her gifts, speaks courteously, is always attentive and thoughtful and takes her out. But so often all of this stops the moment a preacher says, "I now pronounce you man and wife." Many a man never realizes the shock this is to his bride. She is deeply hurt and may even feel betrayed when she realizes that the courtship ended the moment she said, "I do."

It isn't that the young husband (or old husband) does not sincerely love his wife. It is simply that men and women are different and he does not dream how precious and important to her were those little attentions of their courtship days.

Recently on a Saturday evening I was invited to speak at a banquet for ladies in Chattanooga, Tennessee. Bill left early that morning for Texas where he was to begin a revival campaign the next morning. Imagine my surprise, that night, when I stood to speak, to be presented with a gift. When I opened it I found a beautiful, lovely corsage of tiny red rosebuds and a card that read, "You are my Princess. (Signed) Bill."

He had taken time that day on his long drive to wire those flowers to me! I was thrilled from the top of my head to the bottom of my feet. And not only did I receive a thrill, but every woman there was thrilled, too. You never heard so many oh's! and ah's!

Ten years from now I doubt that any woman there will remember a word I said. But you may be sure that every one of them will remember that beautiful red rosebud corsage.

I remember some years ago we were invited to the thirty-fifth wedding anniversary of some dear friends. They were going to have a big dinner with all their family and Bill and I were invited, too.

The wife slaved and worked for several days getting the house nice and clean. Then on the appointed day she was up early cooking and preparing for the "gang" that would be there for the big feast.

A large group was present and all had a happy time celebrating this joyous occasion. When the meal was finished, the husband brought in a large package and handed it to his wife. This lovely woman opened the gift and then her face fell and tears came as she pulled out—a pressure cooker!

The husband dearly loved his bride of thirty-five years and sincerely wanted to give her a nice gift with which she would be pleased. But this lovely woman, I know, felt sick all the way through. No doubt she needed the pressure cooker and the husband should have bought it for her. But not for an anniversary gift. How much better it would have been if he had said, "Our thirty-fifth wedding anniversary is so special—I want you all to myself. On this day I don't want to share you with anyone, not even our children. I am going to buy you the prettiest dress we can find—and the loveliest negligee. And I don't want you cooking or washing dishes today—I am going to take you to a nice restaurant and buy you a steak an inch thick! After that we can go home and spend the evening together—just the two of us."

Perhaps a husband will feel he just doesn't have that kind of money. But if she was worth it before marriage, she should be worth much more after thirty-five years of marriage!

To most men, remembering birthdays and anniversaries and buying gifts is just bother, nonsense and nuisance. Therefore, because most men hate to shop, they just tell the little wife to go and buy whatever she wants for herself. Or he may ask his secretary to get her something. Or, if he does get around to personally selecting a gift, he picks out something practical like a toaster or frying pan!

But women want impractical things for gifts for special occasions—perfume or flowers, a box of candy, lingerie or a new dress.

Bill has always been wonderful to me when it comes to gifts. And it doesn't take an anniversary or a birthday. When he is away in meetings, he nearly always brings something home to me. Sometimes I receive packages in the mail. Or sometimes when he has simply gone to town for something he will stop by a store and get some little gift to surprise me with. In the nature of the case, most of these gifts are inexpensive but I'm always thrilled because I know he is telling me again that I am his sweetheart.

I remember a couple of years ago (this did happen to be my birthday) when Bill was again in Texas and I was home. On my birthday I received a large package. Excited as a kid, I opened it to find several beautifully wrapped packages. They were so pretty I had to show them to everyone in the office and on the Ranch before I opened them. In the boxes I found several beautiful dresses and some lovely, lacy lingerie.

The gifts thrilled me to death. But the fact that he had taken time from his busy revival schedule to shop for these things and had then taken time and pains to see that they were beautifully gift wrapped, meant much more to me.

(I might add here—perhaps other men do not have the taste in clothing to select dresses for their wives. My husband always carries in his wallet a little piece of paper on which is written the size dress, slip, brassiere, stockings and shoes that I wear. Since he knows my size he can surprise me with some article of clothing. Of course it is only fair to say, however, that his taste suits me and this might not work so happily for all husbands and wives.)

2. Some of Your Time.

A wife needs some of her husband's time. Of course most men are busy men. But even if the things they are doing are right and good they are still entirely "too busy" if they do not have time for their wives.

I know and could name many a preacher who is so busy preaching, building a church, solving other people's problems and studying that he actually becomes a stranger to his family. He and his wife grow further and further apart. A man that does not have time for his wife may wake up one day to find that while he was "busy as a bee, his honey has gone."

I have seen women with uncongenial husbands turn to church work, social work, club work or political work for consolation. Or she may find another man who gives her the sympathetic and listening ear she needs. If it turns out he has the same problem in his home, they may soon be telling one another of their mate's coldness and indifference. And this mutual sympathy and understanding can become the Devil's snare to trap them into an ungodly intimacy that ends in shame and disgrace.

But this could have been prevented if only the husband had given his wife the time she so sorely needed.

For a husband and wife to find happiness in their marriage, they *must* be together. Live together, play together, work together, think together and plan together. Marriage cannot be very happy or held together long unless there is a binding force. One sure way for love to grow stronger with the years is for the husband and wife to seek one another's companionship in all phases of their life together; as partners, lovers, friends and companions.

So often a husband, when he thinks of fun and recreation,

will think of one of the men with whom he works rather than of his wife. So often the husband will use the family's spending money on boats and outboard motors, fishing equipment, skin-diving equipment, hunting equipment, bowling equipment, skiing equipment, etc., without making any plans for his wife to enjoy these things with him. Oddly enough, this is more often due to thoughtlessness than any other reason. It simply does not occur to him that his wife, confined to children and household work, simply needs to be *with* him, to bask in the knowledge that he loves her and wants her companionship.

The experience of doing things together makes a couple feel closer together. Remember the Bible says they are *"heirs together of the grace of life."* But more than just time for herself, a wife needs her husband to give time to the home, to take his rightful responsibility regarding the spiritual and secular education of the children; and to give a firm and substantial help in their discipline.

First Timothy 5:8 tells us, *"But if any provide not for his own, and specially for those of his own house, he hath denied the faith, and is worse than an infidel."*

A man's wife should be more important to him than his parents, his best friend, his boss—or anyone else in all the world.

Men need the maturity to accept responsibility. First Corinthians 13:11 says, *"When I was a child, I spake as a child, I understood as a child, I thought as a child: but when I became a man, I put away childish things."*

From what many women tell me, many men, even after marriage, are not willing to give up childish things!

3. Build Her Up.

The happier a man can make his wife, the better wife he is going to have! So, why not build her up?

The fact is, a husband would be absolutely lost without his wife. He needs her for such simple everyday things as preparing the meals, taking care of his clothes, and keeping his house. And he needs her, too, for romance and companionship. A husband, therefore, should express appreciation for hard work and her loving care. He should make her glad she is a woman and that she is his wife.

Since a woman probably spends more time in the kitchen than anywhere else, it is a wise husband who will brag on the food she prepares.

In speaking to my husband, a woman said, "My husband sits down and eats like a hog and never shows any appreciation for the time I spend in preparing his meals. But he is always ready to point out what is wrong."

Now that man was not only being wicked, he was downright stupid. By this time his wife had probably become so discouraged at being unappreciated that she had little desire to please him and likely had no pride in the food she prepared or the way she prepared it.

That husband could certainly learn something from the man I married. I hardly know what it is to prepare a meal that my husband does not brag on and thank me for. And not only my husband but my children as well, for appreciation is contagious just as much as grumbling and complaining is.

Here on the Ranch I do very little "fancy" cooking. We specialize in good, wholesome food. From their babyhood we have taught our children that all food is good and, as a result, I cannot think of one single meat or vegetable that my family does not enjoy. Although none of us are overweight, I will never understand why. My family not only eats heartily but brags on everything they eat!

Again and again, at the close of a meal, my husband will say, "I believe this is the best meal I have ever eaten in all my life." And, although I have heard him say the same thing many times before and will doubtless hear him say the same thing again and again in the future, I always believe it! And it always flatters me to know I have succeeded in pleasing him.

And my heart just sings as I tackle the stacks and stacks of dirty dishes!

The Scripture says, *". . . her husband also. . . praiseth her"* (Prov. 31:28b).

A businessman who appreciates efficiency will compliment his secretary and reward her good work with a raise now and then. Oddly enough, however, it may never occur to that same man to compliment his wife on the efficient way she runs the household, gets the children off to school, sees to it that he always has a supply of fresh clean clothes, is neat and attractive and makes a good impression on his business acquaintances and is an excellent hostess when entertaining his friends.

If a man had to hire a cook, housekeeper, tutor for his children, social secretary and all the other work that his wife does for him, it might well cost him more than his monthly salary! A loving and loyal wife means much to a husband's happiness, well-being and success in life. It is a wise husband, then, who will often tell his wife how much he appreciates her. No husband ever lost by taking time to "build up" his wife!

4. Have Patience With Her.

I know men often say that there is no understanding a woman. They seem to think we are "dizzy blond" creatures. And if the truth be known—we do go in cycles—twenty-eight-day cycles.

A woman is likely to be of a more emotional nature than a man and there are certain times of the month (menstrual) that she may be easily upset. And she may be more prone to worry and more given to tears than her husband. But a husband needs to learn to have patience and to be long-suffering with his wife.

The pressures are often increased for us by the fact that we spend so much of our time at home. Sometimes when the children are sick and we must spend day and night caring for them, it almost seems that we are in solitary confinement. So we need somebody we can let our hair down with and be assured of sympathy and understanding. On trying days the patient, sympathetic understanding of a loving husband certainly helps.

To a husband a wife's complaints may seem trivial, even imaginary. Men are often prone to feel if their wives would only be more practical minded, all these problems would not arise. But God made women different and in spite of how foolish a wife may sometime seem to her husband, the fact is, there are times she needs to cry a little and she needs a loving, kind shoulder to do it on!

When Bill and I were first married we learned the great love chapter, I Corinthians 13, by heart. Notice that it says in part,

"Love suffereth long, and is kind; love envieth not; love vaunteth not itself, is not puffed up, Doth not behave itself unseemly, seeketh not her own, is not easily provoked, thinketh no evil; Rejoiceth not in iniquity, but rejoiceth in the truth; Beareth all things, believeth all things, hopeth all things, endureth all things. Love never faileth.... And now abideth faith, hope, love, these three; but the greatest of these is love."

True love is long-suffering, kind, patient. A husband may not be able to understand why his wife may suffer a feeling of depression or nervousness or crankiness during her menstrual period—but he can and should be sympathetic and patient with her.

5. Love Your Wife and Let Her Know It.

The Bible says, *"Husbands, love your wives"* (Eph. 6:25a). Not only should a husband obey this commandment of God but, by his words and by his actions, he should let her know it. In order to do this there are several important things he should keep in mind.

(a.) Never grow tired of looking at her!

A wife wants to be noticed and she wants to be noticed by her husband more than any other person on earth. It is a well-known fact that in the animal kingdom the male is the most beautiful. The male lion is massive and regal with his huge head and tawny mane, the peacock spreads his glorious tail to attract the hen, the male cardinal is a magnificent scarlet and the buck deer has a royal set of antlers. But in humans it is the female that spends hours trying to beautify herself.

Why?

In order to get that "glance" she so desperately wants and needs. She wants to see approval in her husband's eyes and to know his glance says, "I know you are there—you look beautiful and lovely to me. How I love you. Thank God you are mine!"

No wonder, however, many wives become frowzy, untidy and sloppy. As far as most women are concerned they might as well be a piece of furniture or an old picture hanging on the wall. Many thoughtless husbands never take time to even give their wives a casual glance, much less look at them in love. They either feel there is nothing to look at or else they think they have seen everything there is to see, anyway!

But a man needs to realize that a woman comes alive with radiance and beauty when she sees the man she loves looking at her with love light in his eyes. Without this a wom-an's radiance fades and dies.

When I am in a revival meeting with my husband, I notice he always "looks" for me. When he walks onto a platform and sits down, his eyes begin to search the congregation. When they fall on me, he gives a slight nod, smiles, settles back, opens his Bible and puts his mind and thoughts to the service of the evening. But I feel warm and good all the way through for I have read in his eyes, "There she is—every-thing's all right and I can put my mind on the sermon I'll soon be preaching."

(b.) Love, for a woman, also comes from the warm and loving touch of her husband.

So many men wonder why their wives are not lovers. But to be a lover, a woman must be touched. Every woman wants (and most are starved) to feel the warm and loving touch of her husband's hand on hers. The touch of his hand on her shoulder, the touch of his lips on her cheek, the feel of his arm around her waist. These little "touches" mean so much to a woman's sense of well-being and makes her feel she is just what her husband needs. It is strange that men never seem to realize this important need in a wom-an's life.

But it is easier for a woman to be lovable if she is loved, and a part of loving—for a woman—is being touched by the man she loves.

(c.) Words of love.

A man should never cease giving his wife words of love "as long as ye both shall live." Courtship is never as sweet as among married couples! So why not be as courteous and polite after marriage as in the days of courtship? Words of thanks, words of appreciation, words of love will bring joy to the heart of any wife.

Some men seem never to talk to their wives except to be-rate and tell them how stupidly they manage the house, the children, the money, etc. A woman not only needs a hus-band that she can visit with for companionship but she needs her husband to give her words of loving approval.

If your husband thinks you are especially beautiful in a certain dress, or if he likes your new hair style or if he loves the way you laugh—*he should tell you so!* This will make a wife glad she is alive and happy to be the wife of such a wonderful man. Just knowing that her husband likes the way she looks and acts makes a woman walk more proudly and gives her the desire to improve herself any way she can in his sight.

All husbands would do well to read the Song of Solomon and learn some of his words of love:

"Behold, thou art fair, my love...thou hast doves' eyes ...thy teeth are like a flock of sheep...thy lips are like a thread of scarlet...thy neck is like the tower of David... thou art all fair, my love; there is no spot in thee."

Many a woman has been cruelly hurt because her husband never tells her how much he loves and appreciates her. He probably feels that his hard work in providing her a home and his loyalty to her should be proof enough of his love. But she needs to hear words of love from his own lips.

A woman needs to hear from her husband that she is the most lovely, the sweetest, the most wonderful, the most admired, the most precious, the one person he loves above all others in all the world.

So few men seem to realize that God made women to be creatures of romance. Recently a reporter asked Queen Elizabeth the color of the dress she was wearing. To this the Queen replied, "Well, an ordinary man would probably call it yellow. But women are more romantic, they would call it gold."

And that is exactly right—women *are* romantic. But all the romance and love many women receive comes only from reading love stories or watching soap operas on TV.

* * * * * * * * * * * * * * * * * *

God has created women to be a *"help meet"* for a man. Deep in the heart of every woman is the desire to love, care for and conform to the needs and desires of the one man in her life. Men could reap dividends unlimited if only they would love their wives and let them know it!

"Husbands, love your wives, even as Christ also loved the church, and gave himself for it."—Eph. 5:25.

Chapter 6

The Right Way With Children

*"Lo, children are an heritage of the Lord: and the fruit
of the womb is his reward. As arrows are in the hand of a
mighty man; so are children of the youth. Happy is the man
that hath his quiver full of them: they shall not be ashamed,
but they shall speak with the enemies in the gate."—Ps. 127:
3-5.*

*"Train up a child in the way he should go: and when he is
old, he will not depart from it."—Prov. 22:6.*

It is a thrilling, wonderful and never-to-be-forgotten moment when a precious bundle is placed in the arms of a
woman and she knows this tiny being is her very own!

And what a sense of pride comes to the man when he realizes that he is a father!

Surely all parents should feel like Jacob did so many years
ago when he said to Esau, *"The children which God hath
graciously given thy servant"* (Gen. 33:5b).

Children are really an heritage, a priceless gift from the
Lord.

A GREAT RESPONSIBILITY

Along with the gift of children comes the responsibility of
bringing them up. This is a responsibility we owe to God,
to the children, to the church and to the world. We need to
love them, teach them, train them, win them to Christ and
bring them up to live for God.

This is not an easy task. Not one of us is really smart
enough to know how to raise our children. They are born

knowing absolutely nothing. What they learn must come from us.

I believe most of us women feel so unworthy to be mothers of such precious babies. But we can take comfort and courage from James 1:5 that says, *"If any of you lack wisdom, let him ask of God, that giveth to all men liberally...."*

And Proverbs 2:6 reminds us, *"For the Lord giveth wisdom: out of his mouth cometh knowledge and understanding."*

MUST HAVE LOVE

We often hear the expression, "There is no love greater than the love of a mother." It is true that mother-love is strong. But it should not be a smothering love that gives in to every whim of a child, but a love that causes her to look out for the best interests of her offspring, that makes her want whatever is right and best for the child.

Often a mother will say she cannot punish her child because she loves the child too much. But true love would take the long look. It would look ahead and see what would be best for the child's future. Perhaps the punishment would not make the child's feeling toward you very happy at the moment but in the years to come he will love you for it.

I do not claim to be any special example of what a Christian mother ought to be. When our children were little I often went to bed at night feeling that I had been too strict with them. Many, many times I begged God for wisdom and for help. Bill was gone in revival meetings much of the time and most of the love and discipline and teaching had to come from me.

But I did love my children with all my heart even though I had to be firm with them. And I know today that my children really love me. They tell me so and they show it by their actions.

BETTY   SUPER   KAYE

BETTY RICE CABBAGE   KAYE RICE FITZGERALD

Betty is married to a splendid young preacher, Don Cabbage. They have a baby boy, Jimmy, and are attending Tennessee Temple College in Chattanooga. They will graduate, God willing, in the spring of 1967 and then plan a ministry to the deaf. (Betty is deaf.)

Kaye and Charles met as students at Tennessee Temple but their education was interrupted by the U. S. Marines! They have a lovely baby girl, Cathy, and plan to finish their Christian education when he has finished his hitch in the armed forces.

Recently when I had to have a slight operation, I came home from the hospital on a Friday. Bill had to leave for Texas on Saturday. He hated to leave me but the revival had been scheduled for many months, hundreds of hours had been spent in preparation and hundreds of dollars spent on promotion. I was doing fine and there are several families living here on the ranch that I could turn to for help if I needed it. So I insisted that Bill go on to Texas.

Late Saturday afternoon Pete, our youngest son, came in from Chattanooga where he attends Tennessee Temple College. I was pleased and surprised to see him. When I asked why he came, he said he had come to see how I was getting along and to take care of me. He treated me like a queen and would not let me get up for anything. He waited on me hand and foot.

I was real pleased and flattered with his attentions at the time. Later, however, I learned something that made me even happier. A young man, learning that Pete was home, came by to see him early Sunday morning to ask him to spend the day working with him on a contest. Pete replied he would be in Sunday school that morning but he had not come home to work on a contest but to take care of his mother!

On Valentine's Day I was thrilled to receive a beautiful corsage of tiny red roses from our older son, Bill III, who attends Bob Jones University. I knew it was a sacrifice for him to send the flowers. He works long, hard hours to earn the money that keeps him in college.

Then for Mother's Day I received an orchid with a note that read,

> To my grade school teacher, my high school counselor, my college financier and the most wonderful mother on earth.
>
> (Signed) Bill III.

Now, I do not mean that these were great, earth-shaking events. I could tell scores of such stories about our two girls as well as the two boys. All I am trying to say is that we really do have happiness and fellowship and mutual love in our home.

Our children not only love us; they love the Lord. Each of them was saved at an early age and have been active Christians all of their lives. The two boys, Bill III and Pete, feel called of God to follow in the footsteps of their father as evangelists. Betty is married to a fine young preacher and they feel called of God to work with the deaf. Kaye is married, too, and her husband is still in the Marine Corps. They met at Tennessee Temple College and plan to continue their Christian education as soon as Uncle Sam gives his permission.

But if your children or my children turn out right, it will not be any accident. All children are born the same. All are born in sin and have sinful natures.

Notice the following verses of Scripture that plainly say this is so:

"Behold, I was shapen in iniquity; and in sin did my mother conceive me."—Ps. 51:5.

"The wicked are estranged from the womb: they go astray as soon as they be born, speaking lies."—Ps. 58:3.

"Wherefore, as by one man sin entered into the world, and death by sin; and so death passed upon all men, for that all have sinned."—Rom. 5:12.

Many people who have spoiled brats feel that their children are just more stubborn or have a stronger will than well-behaved children. I have had many say to me, "You have such nice children. But mine are different. You just can't teach my children to obey; they have a mind of their own."

The fact is, however, that all children are born in sin.

All of them have a "mind of their own." Two of our children were stubborn, and two were very stubborn!

That is why children need Christian parents who will *"bring them up in the nurture and admonition of the Lord."*

TEACH THEM TO OBEY

The very first thing God wants you to teach your child is that he is to respect and obey his parents. Never, never, *never* make the mistake of trying to be a "big sister" to your youngster.

So many women seem flattered to death when someone says to them, "You seem more like a big sister than a mother to your children." Actually, you should be insulted rather than pleased. In the first place, the person is probably lying in an attempt to flatter you. In the second place, your child can have someone else for a brother or a sister or a playmate but you are his only chance of having a mother. And, in the third place, children fuss with their "big sisters" and your child should look up to you as one in absolute authority.

I know a woman who used to brag about the fact that she was just a "big sister" to her son. But today he has no respect for his mother whatsoever.

There are a number of Scriptures that stress the fact that children should honor their parents. In fact, the Lord thought this so important that this is the Fifth Commandment:

"Honour thy father and thy mother: that thy days may be long upon the land which the Lord thy God giveth thee."—Exod. 20:12.

This same commandment is repeated in Ephesians 6:2. Because this is so important, little children should be taught from the cradle to respect and obey their parents.

Children who are taught to obey and respect their parents

in the home are more likely to obey authority outside the home: the teacher in the school, the policeman on the beat, the preacher in the pulpit, etc.

And it is far easier to win an obedient child to Christ. My husband at one time had a song leader who had been saved after he was grown. However, he was saved the very first time he ever understood the Gospel. He could have been won to Christ at almost anytime in his life. And, when he gave his testimony, he always said that because of the discipline in his home when he was growing up, he realized his need for salvation the first time he heard of it.

I believe it ought to be a hard-and-fast rule in every home that any child who talks sassy to his mother or father *gets spanked immediately!* I doubt if there is anything more harmful to a child than to permit him to speak to his parents with contempt or even go so far as to strike or kick them.

Let me stress that it is important to begin training your child early. Catholics say that if they have a child until he is seven, he will be a Catholic as long as he lives. And there is a great deal of truth to this. Early teaching is important.

The Bible says, *"Chasten thy son while there is hope, and let not thy soul spare for his crying"* (Prov. 19:18). In other words, chasten him when he is young and it will do the most good.

DEVELOPING CHRISTIAN CHARACTER

Your child will become what you make of him. His character, for better or for worse, depends upon you. From the time he is born until he leaves home, he will be under your roof, at your table and under your authority. How important it is, then, that you take this matter to heart and help your child develop those qualities that will help him and bless others as long as he lives.

1. Good Manners.

Each summer hundreds of teen-age boys and girls come to camp here on the Bill Rice Ranch. And I am absolutely appalled that so few of them ever use the words "thank you" and "please." As for "yes, sir" and "yes, mam"—these must be unknown words altogether!

We were in a revival in New York and some people who had been to the ranch came to the services one night. After church they came around to visit with us. "Do your children," the woman asked, "still say, 'yes, sir' and 'no, sir' and 'yes, mam' and 'no, mam'?" When I assured her that they certainly did, the woman laughed in derision. "That's the silliest thing I ever heard," she said.

Then her husband spoke up. "The only time I ever said, 'yes, sir' to anyone was when I was in the Army. I never did before and I never expect to say 'sir' to anyone again as long as I live."

To this my husband replied, "My friend, I would hate to think it took the whole United States Army to make me speak courteously and respectfully to others! The Bible says we are to give honor to whom honor is due."

"Render therefore to all their dues: tribute to whom tribute is due; custom to whom custom; fear to whom fear; honour to whom honour."—Rom. 13:7.

Perhaps many others feel just as that man and woman felt. But you will rob your children of friends, opportunity and happiness if you do not teach them to speak courteously and politely.

My husband says that using good manners is like using good grammar. The people who do not know any better will not care if you use correct grammar but those who do know better will resent it if you do not.

One of the most beautiful expressions in all the Bible refers to our speech—Proverbs 25:11: *"A word fitly spoken is like apples of gold in pictures of silver."*

Of course courtesy is far more than simply saying "Thank you" and "Yes, sir." Courtesy should really be an outward expression of what we feel in our hearts toward others.

Because we want our child to be unselfish, we should teach him to hold the door for others and allow them to enter before he does. That he may show his respect for womanhood, we should teach him to offer his seat to a lady and to open the car door for his mother and sisters.

Courtesy (or lack of it) reveals character. The Bible says, *"...for out of the abundance of the heart the mouth speaketh"* (Matt. 12:34).

2. Thankfulness.

The Bible says again and again, *"O give thanks unto the Lord."* There is something basically wrong with anyone who is not grateful to God for the many wonderful gifts of life. By all means, teach your children to be thankful.

Ever since Bill and I married we have made it a practice to always thank God for our food. Whether at home, in a hamburger shop, or in the finest restaurant in the land, we always bow our heads and my husband leads in prayer before we eat.

One time we were visiting in Washington, D. C., and the late Senator Tom Connally invited us to eat with him in the Senate dining room. And there, before eating, my husband asked that we bow our heads in prayer. There we sat, Tennessee hillbillies, with all eyes upon us as Bill thanked the Lord for the food!

Of course some people think this custom strange. When someone asked my husband if he doesn't feel embarrassed to pray in public restaurants, he answers, "Shucks, no. Let the fellers who don't pray be embarrassed!"

With our own children, however, it does not seem strange at all. On the contrary, they always thought it so strange that anyone would ever eat without first thanking God for the food.

All of us should realize that everything we have, including the air we breathe, is an undeserved gift from God. James 1:17 says:

"Every good gift and every perfect gift is from above, and cometh down from the Father of lights, with whom is no variableness, neither shadow of turning."

Giving thanks, then, should play a large part in the lives of Christians. Not only should we have thankful hearts toward God but we should show our appreciation to mother, father, loved ones and friends.

In 1964 Bill and I were again in Egypt—a country of real poverty and squalor. We had a good friend in Cairo and we were anxious to see him again. Someone told us the man had died but arrangements would be made for us to meet his family.

We found that the man's wife, mother and several children lived near the Pyramids. Bill and I were so excited. We not only wanted to meet this family but we wanted to be in an Egyptian home.

The house was plain, with very little furniture, though this family is from the high caste of Egypt. But we were so amazed at the politeness and the courtesy of the children. I was especially impressed with the older boy (a teen-ager) who acted as spokesman since his father had died.

He was so well-mannered and so courteous and so thankful. My husband teased me later and said I was impressed because the boy had bowed and kissed my hand!

But I was impressed when he so warmly thanked us for coming to visit in their humble home, for asking about his father's last illness, for inquiring about his education and a number of other things. I knew this was not inborn—he had been well trained by his parents.

Although this was not a Christian home, they were thankful to God for His goodness and their appreciation warmed our hearts.

Being unthankful is mentioned at the beginning of a list of horrible sins in the first chapter of Romans. *"Because that, when they knew God, they glorified him not as God, neither were thankful; but became vain in their imaginations, and their foolish heart was darkened."*

Thankfulness, too, is a matter of Christian character. Teach your child to be thankful in his heart and to express it with his lips.

3. Work.

"Work" has almost become a dirty word in America, especially among our children. But work develops Christian character while laziness is a shame and a disgrace to any person.

In fact, the Bible says that the fellow who is too lazy to work should not be given anything to eat.

"...if any would not work, neither should he eat."—II Thess. 3:10.

On the other hand, work is heartily commended in the Bible time and again.

"Go to the ant, thou sluggard; consider her ways, and be wise."—Prov. 6:6.

"Whatsoever thy hand findeth to do, do it with thy might; for there is no work, nor device, nor knowledge, nor wisdom, in the grave, whither thou goest."—Eccles. 9:10.

Your youngster should learn how to work almost as soon as he learns how to walk. Children are a part of the family and should help with household chores without feeling they are martyrs.

And you will make a real mistake if you let your boy or your girl loaf around in bed all day long. My dad used to say that we sleep one-half of the time anyway, so why sleep three-fourths of our lives away?

"How long wilt thou sleep, O sluggard? when wilt thou a-rise out of thy sleep? Yet a little sleep, a little slumber, a little folding of the hands to sleep: So shall thy poverty come as one that travelleth, and thy want as an armed man."—Prov. 6:9-11.

The following Open Letter to a Teen-ager first received public attention when it was quoted by Juvenile Judge Philip B. Gilliam of Denver. More recently it appeared in Abigail Van Buren's syndicated newspaper column. The author of the letter is not known.

"GO HOME"

We hear Teen-agers complain, "What can we do? Where can we go?" The answer is: Go home! Hang the storm windows, paint the woodwork. Rake the leaves, mow the lawn, shovel the walk. Wash the car, scrub some floors. Visit the sick, the poor. Study your lessons. And you are through; if you're not too tired, read The Book. Your parents do not owe you entertainment. Your city doesn't owe you a recreation center. The world doesn't owe you a living. You owe it your time and energy and your talent so that no one will be at war or in poverty or sick or lonely again. You are supposed to be mature enough to accept some responsibilities your parents have carried for years. They have nursed, protected, excused and tolerated you. They have denied themselves comforts so that you could have luxuries. This they have done gladly, for you are their greatest treasure. Teen-agers, grow up and go home!

What can I add? Enough said!

Our Daily Bread

Of course your boy or girl will probably feel that the tasks you set for him are the very hardest any boy or girl ever had to do in all the history of all the world! Perhaps that is just human nature. But I have never yet known a youngster who enjoyed carrying out trash, washing dishes, mowing the lawn or mopping the floor. But they often tell themselves they wouldn't mind doing the jobs that the neighbor's children have to do.

I will never forget the time I flew to join my husband over the weekend in Toledo, Ohio. My plane landed shortly before church time and so Bill could not meet me at the airport. Friends of ours came, however, with their young son.

The boy was greatly interested in the fact that I lived on a ranch. He complained of the fact that he was a city boy and had spent the day mowing the yard. He hated that but he sure would love to live on a ranch and do the work of a cowboy.

I laughed and then told him that when I left home that morning Pete was saddling up to ride over the Pass and check on the stock. And Pete had complained that he was a ranch boy and had to work so hard riding horses, driving cattle and "stuff like that"! And—Pete had gone on to say that he sure would like to be a city boy who didn't have to do anything but mow the lawn!

But work develops both body and character. You will sin against your child if you do not teach him to work.

4. Dependability.

Every summer we have scores of applications from teen-

98

PETE RICE   SUPER   BILL RICE III

Pete was two and Bill III was four when this picture was taken. Super is older and wiser and looks sadder than when the girls posed with him!

PETE RICE   BILL RICE III

Both boys are preparing to follow the footsteps of their father as evangelists. Pete is a student in Tennessee Temple and Bill III of Bob Jones University. Both take an active part in the summer conferences and general ranch work. Both are soul winners and receive many invitations for revivals and weekend services.

agers who want to come to the Bill Rice Ranch and work during the summer months. And through the years we have hired a good many of them. Usually, however, we do not have them come back another year. The sad fact is, most of them simply are not dependable.

They cannot be trusted to report for work and meals and services promptly. Many of them are simply too lazy to work and they quit after the first week or so. Others will not work unless the boss is standing over them every minute.

We have found that Dr. Bob Jones, Sr., is right when he says, "The greatest ability in all the world is—dependability!"

Our boys and our girls should be taught dependability. We should be able to depend upon them to tell the truth, to be honest, to be on time, to work when they are supposed to work, to play when they are supposed to play, to keep their word and always do what they say they will do.

Several years ago a dark-haired, slender young fellow fourteen years old asked my husband for a job. Bill talked with the boy, explained that it would be hard work and that the pay would be very little. Just the same, the boy was eager for the job and my husband put him on the working crew.

The first evening the boy came to be with us, my husband explained just exactly what his duties would be and what he would be paid. When he had finished the boy said, "Dr. Bill, I would like to be a good worker. I really want to do a good job for you. Does the Bible tell a fellow how to do this?"

My husband sat down on a rail fence with the boy and read these Scriptures:

"Seest thou a man diligent in his business? he shall stand before kings; he shall not stand before mean men."—Prov. 22:29.

"Whatsoever thy hand findeth to do, do it with thy might; for there is no work, nor device, nor knowledge, nor wisdom, in the grave, whither thou goest."—Eccles. 9:10.

"Go to the ant, thou sluggard; consider her ways, and be wise."—Prov. 6:6.

The next morning after breakfast this same boy came around to my husband and said, "Dr. Bill, what would you like for me to do now?"

Bill was a little provoked. "Son," he said, "last night I told you in detail just exactly what I wanted you to do this morning. Now go and do it."

"Oh," the boy said, "I've already done that. I got up this morning about five-thirty and I have already done everything you told me to do today."

My husband checked up and it was the truth! That boy had gotten up before breakfast and had already done everything my husband had expected him to do that day!

So, other work was assigned to the youngster. Bill was very pleased but he was also a little skeptical. It is nothing new to have some boy try to "impress" the boss.

But this boy wasn't trying to impress anyone. He continued to work like he was fighting fire! After a couple of weeks my husband doubled his salary. A few weeks later he increased his salary again. And again.

Needless to say, that young fellow comes back to the ranch every summer and has become one of our most valued helpers. What's more, he now receives enough pay that it will go a long way toward putting him through college.

Every summer there are other teen-age boys who envy this young fellow. Most of them believe that he simply got "the breaks." The truth is, however, that we feel we are the ones who really got "the breaks"—for having a young man like this help us in the work we are trying to do.

"Therefore, my beloved brethren, be ye stedfast, unmove-
able, always abounding in the work of the Lord, forasmuch
as ye know that your labour is not in vain in the Lord."—
I Cor. 15:58.

SALVATION

When a tiny baby is born, the mother and father are so
thankful and so proud. Announcements are sent out to all
the relatives and friends telling whether it is a boy or girl,
how much it weighed at birth, and what its name is.

And immediately the mother and father begin planning for
the future of their baby. Isn't it strange, though, that this
"future" hardly ever has anything to do with the child's salvation and Christian training? The fact is, even Christians
evidently do not put spiritual training on a par with the
child's secular education. What parents, when the baby is
born, begin planning what Bible stories they will first read
to the little one, what Sunday school teachers they would
like to have teach him or just how soon they hope to be able
to get the child saved?

Incidentally, we send out announcements when the baby is
born. But do parents ever send out announcements to the
family and friends when the child has been saved, has been
born again?

Your child's salvation is the single most important thing
in his life.

1. Our Responsibility.

We are so anxious that our children be well educated. But
we just "hope" that they will be saved. We just "suppose"
that if we take them to Sunday school fairly regularly and to
church once in a while, someone will surely get them saved.

But their salvation is not the responsibility of a preacher

or Sunday school teacher nearly as much as it is our own responsibility. Both God and man hold us accountable for our children's salvation. And this is right. Do not take it for granted, then, that someone else will do this job for us.

Joshua, in a land surrounded by heathen, said:

"...choose you this day whom ye will serve...but as for me and my house, we will serve the Lord."—Josh. 24:15.

Joshua took full responsibility for his own family. We should take the full responsibility for our families. And to do that we must begin early and simply saturate our children with the Scriptures.

"And these words, which I command thee this day, shall be in thine heart: And thou shalt teach them diligently unto thy children, and shalt talk of them when thou sittest in thine house, and when thou walkest by the way, and when thou liest down, and when thou risest up. And thou shalt bind them for a sign upon thine hand, and they shall be as frontlets between thine eyes. And thou shalt write them upon the posts of thy house, and on thy gates."—Deut. 6:6-9.

God commanded the Israelites to teach their children *"diligently."* They were to talk about the Word of the Lord constantly: when they sat down, when they were walking around, when they lay down, when they got up again! And they were to wear the Word of God on their heads, on their hands, have it on the walls of their houses and on their gates.

We need to have Bible reading in the home, prayer at the table, Bible stories at night and remind our children constantly of the goodness of God toward us.

Our first child, Betty, was deafened by meningitis when she was almost two years old. Of course we were broken-hearted that our little girl must go through life deaf. But I was so concerned that she be saved. I did not know anything about teaching the deaf but I felt it would be unpardonable if my husband won souls around the world and our one little deaf girl was unsaved!

I wrote to everyone I could think of asking for help. But of all the denominational headquarters I contacted, only one had anything at all for me. That was a Sunday school quarterly for adult deaf.

I realized, with a fearful heart, that if Betty was going to learn anything about the Lord Jesus Christ it must come from us. I prayed to the Lord for wisdom and then set out to see what I could do.

We took Betty to Sunday school and church all the time but of course she got nothing out of it. I am sure she saw pictures on the walls of the Sunday school rooms representing Jesus, but how could a little deaf girl know who He was?

When Betty was three years old she started to school, a school for little deaf children. So her secular education had begun. But she still knew nothing about the Bible or God.

When Betty was five years old I bought a blackboard, a scrapbook and stories of the Bible told in pictures. I cut out pictures and pasted them in the scrapbook, pictures of little boys and girls, men and women, puppy dogs and kitty cats, woolly lambs and shepherd boys, the sun and moon and stars, etc. Then we started learning from these. Every night we would have a Bible lesson.

Although Betty was deaf, she had learned to read a little. And, fortunately, it developed that she had an unusual talent for lip-reading.

I began in Genesis with the Story of Creation. With a blackboard, scrapbook and Bible story books I taught as best I could through drawing pictures, acting things out and anything else I could do to make Betty understand about God, about the teaching of the Bible and about ourselves.

These lessons were a nightly affair. And I mean "nightly." Every night of the world, after supper, we would go into our large living room and begin what my husband called my "Home Bible Conference."

In the meantime Kaye, our second daughter, had been born. She was two years old when these Bible lessons began and so she joined the happy "congregation." And they really were happy times. The children looked forward to them. I spent a great deal of time and tears and prayer in the preparation of these lessons.

One night when Betty was eight years old I taught about Jesus dying on the cross for us. Betty looked at me and said, in her halting speech, "Mother, I love Jesus. Mother, I want Jesus."

This was heavenly music to my ears! This is what I had been working and praying for through these three years. How thankful I was to God that He had heard and answered my prayer and that my precious little deaf girl was saved!

Remember Kaye had been sitting in these classes, too. She was now five years old. She looked up and said, "Mother, I love Jesus, too! Can I be saved?"

I was taken by surprise. Actually, I had been working on Betty and had not realized that a five-year-old child, if carefully taught, might be saved as readily as a child of eight or even older.

I hurriedly answered, "Certainly, Kaye, you can be saved, too!"

Then I gathered both of my little girls in my arms as we knelt and prayed, thanking God for their salvation.

The next thing I did was rush to the telephone to tell my husband, who was conducting a revival in a northern state, the good news.

Both of our boys, too, were saved at an early age. Bill III

was not quite six years old when he was saved in the kitchen of our home. Pete was not quite five when I led him to Christ. Again, it was in the kitchen.

2. Win Them While They Are Young.

Most children are ready to be saved long before we are ready to try to win them!

Many a time I have seen a pastor actually embarrassed because a little child came forward in response to the invitation. I have even heard preachers apologize for a little fellow six or seven or eight years of age saying he wanted to be saved. And I am afraid many parents discourage little children from being saved.

Actually, however, they should be saved while they are young. They are ready.

When little children came to Jesus, the disciples were distressed. But Jesus said:

". . . Suffer the little children to come unto me, and forbid them not: for of such is the kingdom of God. "—Mark 10:14.

And lest anyone should think that Jesus was not talking about these little children being saved, read the next verse.

"Verily I say unto you, Whosoever shall not receive the kingdom of God as a little child, he shall not enter therein." —Mark 10:15.

As a matter of fact, there is a sense in which *only* children can be saved! If one is not saved when he is a child, then he must go back and become as a little child in order to be saved!

Besides, why would any of us want our precious children to live in sin for some years before winning them to Christ? Why take a chance on their hearts becoming so hardened by the enticements of sin that they might never be saved? Or what if your child should die before he is won to Christ?

Please believe me, as the wife of an evangelist, I do know that these things do happen.

Some dear friends of ours had a beautiful little girl. When she was about five years old she said she wanted to be saved. At first they thought she was too young but the child kept insisting she wanted to be saved. She talked of Jesus all the time.

Finally, the parents sat down with the little girl and carefully explained to her the plan of salvation. In the home she trusted in Jesus. Then, in church, the little girl went forward to publicly profess her faith in Christ. She joined the church and was baptized.

Just a few months later a peculiar disease struck this beautiful little girl with the golden hair. In a short time she lost the power to speak. Gradually she began to lose much of her equilibrium and walking became difficult.

Although her splendid parents took her to the finest specialists, doctors could do nothing for little Darlene. Gradually the child became so feeble that she had to be moved in a wheel chair.

She reached her early teens before she died and Bill was asked to preach the funeral.

I have heard both of her parents say, again and again and again, how thankful they were that they had won their little daughter to Christ at such an early age.

3. Raise Them to Live for God.

It is so important to win your children to Christ. But this is the beginning, not the ending, of your responsibility. It is important now to bring them up so they will live for the Lord.

". . .but bring them up in the nurture and admonition of the Lord."—Eph. 6:4b.

I had a dear friend who was so thrilled when her eight-year-old boy was saved. She told me, "Now I can relax and take it easy. My boy has been saved and I don't have anything more to worry about."

But I told her she was mistaken. The fact that a child is saved is no guarantee that he will live for Christ. Even Paul, the great apostle, was concerned lest he be a *"castaway."*

The children of Israel were solemnly warned, *"Then beware lest thou forget the Lord, which brought thee forth out of the land of Egypt, from the house of bondage"* (Deut. 6:12).

Our children should be taught Bible truth and be grounded in the Christian faith. And this teaching should be done consistently, day in and day out. There should be Bible reading and prayer in the home every day. The entire family should go to church every time the doors are open—Sunday morning, Sunday night, Wednesday night and special meetings.

It really is true, as the psalmist said, that the Bible is a protection against sin.

"Thy word have I hid in mine heart, that I might not sin against thee."—Ps. 119:11.

"Thy word is a lamp unto my feet, and a light unto my path."—Ps. 119:105.

The very first Psalm says we are not to walk, stand or sit with evil,

"But his delight is in the law of the Lord; and in his law doth he meditate day and night."—Ps. 1:2.

Many times I have heard my husband tell about his boyhood in West Texas. Every night the family would gather around the fireplace where they often had popcorn, more often enjoyed cowboy stories from Bill's father and always had Bible reading and prayer. Before my husband was old enough to go to school he already knew just about every Bible story he knows today. He was saved when he was nine years old and by the time he was twelve, he was thoroughly familiar with major Bible doctrines.

And those Bible studies really paid off in the years to come, for Bill's parents died when he was in his early teens.

He was thrown among rough, ungodly men when he worked as water boy for threshing crews on the big ranches. And, of course, he faced the same temptations that every boy and girl face in high school and college.

And he was entirely on his own. He could have done anything he wanted to do. There wasn't a person on earth to boss him.

Time and again Bill was urged to go into sin by his classmates. And again and again he was tempted.

But Bill did not yield to these temptations. He never went to a single dance. He never tasted a single drop of booze. He never committed adultery. He never smoked or gambled. And yet many of his classmates did all of these things. Many times he wanted to go along with them but everytime he would remember *"...Whatsoever a man soweth, that shall he also reap." "...Be sure your sin will find you out." "...the wages of sin is death,"* and the stories of David, of Samson, of Peter and others whose sins found them out.

Instead of going into sin, Bill went into the pulpit! And this, as I have heard him say again and again, was a direct result of the Bible teaching in his home during his boyhood days.

Let me close this chapter by urging you not to take the spiritual welfare of your children for granted. I am sure all of us are familiar with Bible stories of great men whose children went wrong. And I could tell you of some of the most famous preachers America has ever produced whose children have gone wrong, who are living in sin and breaking the hearts of their parents.

If your children turn out to be men and women whose lives glorify God, it will not be any "happen-so." It will be because of the way you brought them up.

And if your children turn out to be the kind who live in sin and break your heart—that will not be any accident, either. That, too, will be because of the way you brought them up.

Face this truth and determine in your heart that you will...

"Train up a child in the way he should go: and when he is old, he will not depart from it."—Prov. 22:6.

With my husband and the John Rices on the ocean liner Italia, sailing the Atlantic.

Chapter 7

The Right Later Years

"And be ye kind one to another, tenderhearted, forgiving one another, even as God for Christ's sake hath forgiven you."—Eph. 4:32.

"The aged women likewise, that they be in behaviour as becometh holiness, not false accusers, not given to much wine, teachers of good things; That they may teach the young women to be sober, to love their husbands, to love their children, To be discreet, chaste, keepers at home, good, obedient to their own husbands, that the word of God be not blasphemed."—Titus 2:3-5.

Every year your marriage should grow stronger and sweeter. Anyone is mistaken who believes that the delights and joys of marriage are only for the young. The years after the children are grown and gone from home can be the best years of all.

One of the most interesting stories in the Bible is found in Genesis 12, the story of Abraham's sin in lying to the people of Egypt. And yet there is something strangely beautiful and touching in the story, too, if you remember that Abraham was already seventy-five years old.

Because of the famine in the land of Palestine, Abraham and Sarah went into the land of Egypt.

"And it came to pass, when he was come near to enter into Egypt, that he said unto Sarai his wife, Behold now, I know that thou art a fair woman to look upon: Therefore it shall come to pass, when the Egyptians shall see thee, that they shall say, This is his wife: and they will kill me, but they will save thee alive. Say, I pray thee, thou art my sister:

that it may be well with me for thy sake; and my soul shall live because of thee."—Gen. 12:11-13.

Abraham felt that his wife was so beautiful and so desirable that every Egyptian would want her for his own. Here Sarah was sixty or past—yet to Abraham she was the most attractive and glamorous creature on earth! He even feared for his own life because of the beauty of his wife. And later on we see this very same thing happen again.

In the 17th chapter of Genesis God told Abraham that he would have a son. To this Abraham laughed and said, *"Shall a child be born unto him that is an hundred years old? and shall Sarah, that is ninety years old, bear?"*

Abraham may have felt Sarah too old to have a child but he still thought her so beautiful and attractive that some other man might even kill him to take her! And this fear may have been well grounded. Sarah really was such a beautiful woman that she was desired by King Abimelech.

It seems to me there is a wonderful lesson for both husbands and wives in this story.

In the first place, I wonder if Sarah did not retain her beauty and charm and attractiveness partly because of a husband who was still a fervent sweetheart and lover. And in the second place, I wonder if Abraham was not such a devoted husband because Sarah put him first in her love and loyalty.

In any case, we know that Sarah was a wonderful wife because God used her, in I Peter 3:4-6, as an example of what a Christian wife should be.

"But let it be the hidden man of the heart, in that which is not corruptible, even the ornament of a meek and quiet spirit, which is in the sight of God of great price. For after this manner in the old time the holy women also, who trusted in God, adorned themselves, being in subjection unto their own husbands: Even as Sara obeyed Abraham, calling him lord:

whose daughters ye are, as long as ye do well, and are not afraid with any amazement."

RIGHT LIVING BEGETS LOVE

One time when I was teaching a class on marriage and mentioned Sarah, a woman in the class said, "Sarah is no example to me. After all, in Eastern countries parents arranged the marriages and there is no love involved."

But this is not necessarily so. I have learned, from visiting Eastern countries, that even when parents arrange the marriages, the couple will fall in love when both the man and the woman do right.

Bill and I have a good friend in Cairo, Egypt. He was our guide on one of our visits there and was to be married soon after our departure. I was interested in his being so excited about the marriage when I knew his parents had arranged it. I asked him if he loved the girl and he frankly answered no, he hardly knew her!

But, he went on to explain, he expected to fall in love with her if she made him the right kind of wife.

And, sure enough, that is the way it turned out. He has just written us to tell of the birth of a fourth baby son! In his letter he said, "Perhaps you would like to know that I am now married and have four sons. God has just blessed our humble home with the fourth boy. My wife is all I expected in marriage. My love is great for her. Allah is gracious to us."

AN ACHIEVEMENT

As I have said before in this book, a happy marriage is not an accident, it is an achievement. I remember one time hearing a man say that he and his wife would soon be married fifty years. When someone asked if they were still in love, he answered, with a serious face, "No, we are not in love, we are still climbing into it!"

After fifty wonderful years of marriage they were still working to make it a happy one.

Anytime you see a happily married couple you can know it is not just a happen-so but it is the result of a full-time job.

A woman once said that being married was like a big banquet and then settling down to bread and beans. You marry and go on a honeymoon and that is like a big banquet. Then you go home and settle down and life becomes a bread-and-bean existence. According to her, the only exciting and thrilling and romantic thing about marriage is the first few days.

Some marriages may be like that but no marriage need be. Your marriage does not have to be a boring affair—it can be one continual honeymoon.

BIBLE HELPS FOR MARRIAGE PROBLEMS

1. When You Quarrel.

All married people should be fully aware of troubles and dangers that tend to break down marriage. Paul was referring to this when he said:

"...if thou marry, thou hast not sinned; and if a virgin marry, she hath not sinned. Nevertheless such shall have trouble in the flesh: but I spare you."—I Cor. 7:28.

The Devil is happy if he can wreck and ruin your marriage and make your home unfit for raising children. Perhaps quarreling is the most dangerous and destructive habit a married couple can fall into.

Quarreling is like decay that begins from within. But if we are aware of this danger, we can be prepared for it. We need to pray for ourselves and for each other and learn to guard our heart and lips.

A tremendous recipe for happiness and joy in marriage may be found in I Peter 3:8,9:

"Finally, be ye all of one mind, having compassion one of another, love as brethren, be pitiful, be courteous: Not rendering evil for evil, or railing for railing: but contrariwise blessing; knowing that ye are thereunto called, that ye should inherit a blessing."

If you have love for life and want happy days, then you need to constantly control your tongue and work for peace and harmony.

Sometimes it may seem almost impossible to avoid a quarrel but, remember, it still takes two to fight! Any wife (or husband) will find the advice of Proverbs 15:1 worth its weight in gold:

"A soft answer turneth away wrath: but grievous words stir up anger."

The plain truth is, a wife can go a long way toward avoiding a quarrel if she will simply keep her mouth shut when trouble is brewing! Proverbs 21:23 says, *"Whoso keepeth his mouth and his tongue keepeth his soul from troubles."*

When a quarrel is brewing, the wife and husband need to learn to talk to one another and work things out. Sometimes it may be wise to simply drop the issue until a "cooling-off" period has lapsed! In any case, each should be ready to forgive the other as freely as Christ forgave us. We need to learn to be kind, tenderhearted and forgiving toward one another.

Many a quarrel could be averted if just one member of the marriage team works at Hebrews 10:24:

"And let us consider one another to provoke unto love and to good works."

Of course it is always best if both husband and wife cooperate in everything. But, let me repeat, just one of the two can go a long way toward building a happy marriage. But the effort must be a consistent one.

I am afraid many women feel about this matter like a man did about tithing. He said he did not believe in giving a tenth to the Lord. He did not believe that God blessed those who did. When asked if he had ever tried tithing, he replied that he certainly had—he one time gave the tithe from two pay checks! And it hadn't done him a bit of good as far as he could tell!

But actually, this man did not prove anything about tithing. He did, however, prove something about himself! He proved that he was not willing to do what God wanted him to do.

There are some women who are like that in their marriages. Their home is unhappy and they decide they will begin living according to the teaching of the Bible. But after just two or three days, if she does not see a revolutionary change in her husband, she gives up. Her attitude is, "What's the use? It won't work anyway."

There are two things wrong with this attitude. In the first place, the wife ought to do right whether the husband does or not. In the second place, the woman who really practices the Bible way in marriage will find that it does work.

One summer here on the ranch a woman in my class heard me say that the wife should do right whether the husband did or not. And this woman was very indignant. She told me she had tried to be sweet and kind and loving but the sweeter she was, the meaner he became! Later, however, she heard me tell the story of the man who knew that tithing did not work because he had tried it for two whole weeks! This woman came back to me to say that I had really hit the nail on the head and she was convicted because she had never really given God a fair chance to help her work things out in her marriage.

She said, "Oh, I would try a day or two but my husband stayed so mean and hateful that I would always go back to my old way. But with God's help I want to get my heart right and I'm going to do everything I can for as long as it takes to make my marriage the right kind."

_ 2. In-law Trouble.

As I mentioned in chapter 3, trouble with in-laws plays a major part in approximately 65% of the divorces in America. And of these, approximately 55% of the time the in-law causing the trouble is the husband's mother!

The parents of the bride and groom should certainly try to be helpful but they should also realize they help the most when they interfere the least.

We are commanded to honor father and mother and we do have responsibilities to our parents. But when we marry, we have taken on a new home, a new life, new responsibilities and new loyalties.

So husband and wife should come first in the minds and hearts of each other. Husband and wife should present a united front. They should never allow anything or anyone to separate them.

Jesus said, *"What therefore God hath joined together, let not man put asunder."*

It is right for us to love our parents with all our hearts but for harmony and a happy marriage, husband and wife must be loyal to one another and allow neither in-laws nor parents to cause friction between themselves.

3. Finances.

How the family finances are to be handled is another major cause of unhappiness between wives and husbands. But here, as in other matters, difficulties should be frankly discussed.

Amos 3:3 says, *"Can two walk together, except they be agreed?"*

There needs to be a mutual agreement on running the finances of the home. While it is true that the man is the head of the house, the wife should not be humiliated by having to constantly ask for money like a little child begging for pennies.

Since my husband and I see alike on money matters, we have a joint banking account. Even then, we usually discuss the purchase of anything that costs more than just a few dollars.

If this does not seem best in your case, then your husband should set aside a portion of his paycheck for you to use on household and personal expenses. Nothing is more likely to sow the seed of dishonesty than a woman being tempted to withhold from the grocery money or to pick from her husband's pockets.

Certainly a well-balanced budget should be planned. Otherwise, you are likely to find that your money has been spent and your running expenses and household bills are still unpaid.

And speaking of the budget, always remember that the Lord's portion belongs to Him first.

"...the tithe...is the Lord's."—Lev. 27:30.

The remainder is entrusted to you—as a couple—to administer. Don't say, "This is mine," or "That is yours," but "This is ours."

Learn to live within your means and keep out of debt as much as possible. Romans 13:8 says, *"Owe no man any thing, but to love one another."*

In the first place, if you pay cash for what you buy, your money will certainly go farther.

In the second place, if you get in debt without having anything to show for it, you may lose your reputation for honesty and it may take you years to recover your name.

Of course it may be well to buy an automobile or a home on time since the property will be security for the debt. But

it is not wise to go into debt for anything that you use up—
groceries, gasoline, medicines, etc.

In the third place, the pressure of debts often lead to a
sense of frustration, irritability, and just plain crankiness!

4. Children.

The Bible says that children are a heritage of the Lord
and *"Happy is the man that hath his quiver full of them."*

In most cases, children tend to bind husband and wife together. But children can sometimes make trouble in a home.
Occasionally the organization of a home is broken down because there is not mutual agreement over the discipline and
rearing of children.

This must not be. Husband and wife should guard against
Satan playing one party to the marriage against the other
through the children.

Here again, husband and wife need to be in complete a-
greement and should talk this matter out. They should come
to a thorough understanding as to what is to be expected of
the children.

The children should be made to understand that there is a
complete agreement between mother and dad as to the discipline in the home. Neither parent should try to curry
favor with the children at the expense of the other. Sons
and daughters should never be allowed to come between
husband and wife.

ALWAYS HIS SWEETHEART

Being taken for granted is a termite that eats into a marriage and soon wrecks the romance, the brightness, the
warmth and the love that should be maturing and growing
stronger as the years roll by. As said before, happiness in
a marriage does not come automatically but is the dividend
for doing the right thing, at the right time, in the right way,
with the right motive.

1. Keep Neat and Attractive.

Sarah must have kept herself neat and attractive. Her husband felt she was a real beauty after ninety years of age. But how many of us work to maintain and keep our personal attractiveness for our husbands?

First Peter 3 tells us not to let our dress or adorning be the main thing in our lives. The main thing should be the attitude of our hearts. All the beautiful dressing and adorning will be of no avail if we have a mean and hateful spirit.

But it is still true that if our heart is right toward the one we love, then we should certainly be anxious to keep ourselves as physically attractive as possible. The picture of a beautiful and lovely wife as found in Proverbs 31:22 says, *"She maketh herself coverings of tapestry; her clothing is silk and purple."*

Here is an example for us. I do not know if the silk refers to lingerie but we should certainly keep our underclothing dainty and fresh.

And we should be as anxious to dress neatly after marriage as before. This does not necessarily mean extravagance in the purchase of clothing. But real care and taste should be exercised. A hem taken up or let down as the case may be will keep your present clothing in style. Every man wants to be proud of his wife and I believe most men admire a well-groomed, neatly clad woman.

It is surprising how little difference there may be in a woman who looks well groomed and one who looks untidy. And it might be something as easily corrected as lint on a coat or a slip at half-mast.

So keep yourself looking neat and attractive for your husband.

2. Keep Your Body Clean.

We should do all that we can to keep ourselves nice from

the skin out. As a woman grows older and especially as she enters the menopause, she is likely to be more prone to body odor. A frequent bath is advisable to keep the body clean and sweet-smelling at all times. A nice fresh toilet water, cologne or powder will help.

We all read and chuckle over the ads about halitosis. But halitosis is no joke! A bad breath may even make conversation unpleasant and it certainly is no aid to love and romance.

Remember, wives, it pays to keep kissable!

3. Hair Attractively Worn.

If you won the love and affection of your husband by wearing your hair in pin curls, brush rollers, bobby pins and other like contraptions, then I'd advise you to keep it up. But most men I know hate to see women with their hair rolled up on top of their heads.

First Corinthians 11:15 says, *"But if a woman have long hair, it is a glory to her: for her hair is given her for a covering."*

One of the most noticeable differences between a man and a woman is their hair. It is a sign of feminity and your husband will appreciate it if you keep your hair neat, clean and attractively worn.

Usually "way-out" hair styles are not appreciated by men. The woman who tries to imitate the latest Hollywood hair fashions is more likely to look like a freak than a glamour girl!

But it is just as bad not to keep your hair neatly brushed and combed and styled. No woman can really be attractive to her husband (or to anyone else) if her hair looks stringy or greasy or tousled or dirty. Your hair should be kept neat, clean and attractively worn.

But try to "wash and set" it in the absence of your hus-

band when possible. I know there are times and circumstances when you cannot do this. But you can let your husband know that you are fixing your hair so as to look nice
for him.

I know this takes daily care and trouble. My husband says
the first question I will ask when I get to Heaven is whether
or not the climate up there will make my hair stringy!

Just the same, if your hair looks nice for your husband it
will be worth all the time and trouble. Who knows—he may
run his fingers through it while he holds you in his arms!

4. Watch Your Weight.

I know this is a "ticklish" subject because we all love to
eat. I realize, too, that weight is more of a problem to
some women than to others. But we need to discipline ourselves and keep neat and trim.

Those extra pounds cannot help and they may do much
harm. Certainly you will not enjoy life as well if you are
very much overweight and you may die years earlier than
you otherwise would.

It's a well-known fact that when too fat you tire more
easily, the heat hurts you more, you are more subject to
heart trouble and you don't feel as well.

And, let's face facts: clothes just do not look as well on
you with extra pounds as they did when you had less weight.

Perhaps it is natural for an overweight woman to feel that
she simply gains more easily than others. And, of course,
this may be partially true. The fact remains, however, that
almost any of us will gain weight after thirty-five unless we
take care of our bodies.

My husband is always bragging about the fact that I only
weigh three pounds more today than I did on our wedding
day. (I am five feet, four inches tall, weigh 115 pounds.)
But the fact that I am the same size today as I was when we

With my grandbabies Jimmy and Cathy at my desk on the Bill Rice Ranch.

were married is certainly no accident. For years I could eat anything and everything without gaining a pound. But today I would really get fat if I just let myself go. I have found that it is far easier to keep pounds off than it is to lose them after you get them.

Good Housekeeping Magazine says one out of every five men is overweight, and one out of every four women is overweight.

Every overweight person is anxious for some magic and quick way to lose pounds. Everyone wants a pill that will melt fat while they eat all they want.

Americans spend one hundred million dollars a year on weight-reducing pills!

But doctors say there is no safe product today that, by itself, will cause a person to lose fat gained from overeating. The only safe way to weigh less is to eat less.

You can't lose weight without real work. As my brother-in-law, Dr. John R. Rice, says, it takes real character to lose weight!

But it can be done if you will cut down on your eating.

Someone has said we should eat like a king in the morning, a nobleman at noon, and a pauper at night. In other words, hearty, medium and light!

I know this will be hard. And it may be complicated because you must take other members of your family into consideration. I know this better than almost anyone because, believe me, I have a real problem. My husband likes to eat a big meal every night after church! (He never eats in the evening before preaching.)

But if you have pride in your husband's wife, you will not mind the hardship and you will reap real joy and satisfaction for yourself and for your husband.

You must watch yourself constantly to keep from falling into the rut of taking your husband's love and admiration for granted. When this is allowed to happen, you will soon let yourself go and attractiveness and physical charm will be a thing of the past. I have heard some men say that they do not care how fat their wives get. But—you know what?—I just don't believe them!

5. Don't Live in the Past.

One of the most pathetic and heart-rending persons is one who lives in the past. We often see women, sad and lonely, living on past glories when the children were still at home. But God gave the command, *"Therefore shall a man leave his father and his mother, and shall cleave unto his wife: and they shall be one flesh."*

A woman's heart should be completely filled with love for her husband even after the children are grown and married.

The greatest thrill to the heart of a woman is to have a

precious little bundle placed in her arms and to know that this is her baby. And there is a great sense of fulfillment to a man to know that he is a father. But all parents should realize that their babies are given to them for a time to train, mold and direct into Christian manhood and woman-hood. Then they will be gone to establish their own homes.

We cannot keep our sons and daughters always. This is not right. I have seen young men and women whose lives have been warped and ruined by a "loving mother." Some women even manage to have a "heart attack" every time the young one tries to leave home.

Life moves forward and we cannot keep the past with us. So, don't try.

Memories are precious, but we must live today. Paul said:

"...but this one thing I do, forgetting those things which are behind, and reaching forth unto those things which are before, I press toward the mark for the prize of the high calling of God in Christ Jesus."—Phil. 3:13, 14.

If we live to see our children grown and happily estab-lished, we should thank God for granting us this blessed privilege. It is good to have happy memories of the past but it is better to be content with the present. Like Paul, we should learn *"...in whatsoever state I am, therewith to be content"* (Phil. 4:11).

An old man was asked if he hated growing old. He replied he did not—he must either be old or dead and he would rath-er be old!

I read recently of Shirley Temple's move into her new and palatial home. When the movers came they found trunks and boxes loaded with mementos of her life as a child star. These were all stored in the garage with the mice and the rats!

One of the movers said to her, "Why, Miss Shirley, you

should not have all of these things stored out here; they ought to be on display in a specially built room. These placards, souvenirs and news releases deserve a better place than being tucked away in the garage."

Shirley told him she was very proud of her early years when she had been the most famous child star in history. Those had, indeed, been years of glory. But they were in the past and she was living in the present, she said. She had found her life with a fine husband and lovely children just as rewarding. She had no regrets.

When I read that, I thought of something Jesus said, *"...for the children of this world are in their generation wiser than the children of light"* (Luke 16:8b).

Be grateful that God has permitted you to live until now and make the most of your days. Psalm 118:24 says, *"This is the day which the Lord hath made; we will rejoice and be glad in it."*

My mother told me that the last twenty-five years, since my sisters and I have been gone from home, have been wonderful years for her. She said they have been carefree and she has been able to live a full and rewarding life. She teaches a large women's Bible class, is in great demand as a speaker and has many other worthwhile activities.

And that is right and good and the way it should be.

Paul says in Colossians 3:23, *"And whatsoever ye do, do it heartily, as to the Lord...."* So make every year of your marriage full and rewarding and live it *"heartily"* as to the Lord.

6. Be an Example and Teacher.

We need to set examples, not only before our own children, but before other young people that they may copy us in good and holy marriages.

"The aged women likewise, that they be in behaviour as

*becometh holiness, not false accusers, not given to much
wine, teachers of good things; That they may teach the young
women to be sober, to love their husbands, to love their
children, To be discreet, chaste, keepers at home, good,
obedient to their own husbands, that the word of God be not
blasphemed,"—Titus 2:3-5.*

The old saying, "What you are speaks so loud I cannot
hear what you say," is so true. The way you and your husband live before your children will have a tremendous influence on the kind of marriage your sons and daughters will
have. Many boys and girls grow up in such a fussy, nagging,
cranky atmosphere that it becomes a way of life for them.
When they marry, their homes have a tendency to become
the same.

No better words can be said of a woman than the words of
Proverbs 31:28, *"Her children arise up, and call her blessed; her husband also, and he praiseth her."*

TWO THINGS TO CONSIDER

In closing this chapter, may I make two simple observa-
tions.

First, out of all the girls in the world, your husband chose
you. You are the one he courted. You are the one he married. You are the one he loved with all his heart. So, ex-
amine your heart and do everything you can to always be
that same, sweet person he married. Do this for his sake.
And do it for your own. After all, your only hope for romance and intimate love is with your own husband.

In the second place, you are just going to live here on
this earth in the flesh one time. So, why not make the most
of every single day? Do not wait until next year or next
month or even next week to be the kind of sweetheart and
wife both God and your husband expect you to be.

Begin right now!

CASSETTE TAPES AVAILABLE FROM
THE BILL RICE RANCH
Murfreesboro, TN 37130

BY DR. BILL RICE—

Marriage—Husbands and Wives
Love 'em, Lick 'em and Learn 'em
Morning-glories
What You Have Is Enough
Don't Be a Baby Christian
David's Sin, Our Warning
Second Coming
Judgment
Hell

BY DR. CATHY RICE—

The Right One in Marriage
The Right Plan in Marriage
The Right Sex in Marriage
The Right Dress for Teenage Girls
What Boys Like
What Boys Don't Like
Seven Golden Teen Years
Understanding the Deaf
Problems of a Preacher's Wife

Write for a complete listing of Ranch tapes available.
Price: **$4.00** each.